Educating Handicapped Children

THE LEGAL MANDATE

Reed Martin

Research Press Company
2612 North Mattis Avenue
Champaign, Illinois 61820

To Joan

my colleague in advocacy

Contents

Preface

Many of the legal citations in this book refer to material unfamiliar to the lay reader. Court cases are noted in the text by their popular names and the full citation is given in References. An attorney or librarian can help find any case the reader is interested in. Legal periodicals, such as the United States Code Congressional and Administrative News (cited as U.S. Code Cong. and Ad. News), can also be found easily if the citation is shown to a lawyer or librarian.

The Appendix contains excerpts from relevant federal regulations. Material was omitted which related more to bureaucratic administrative problems than to potential areas of conflict between parent and school. Any reader who wishes to see omitted portions can find them in Volume 45 of the Code of Federal Regulations, which is available in most libraries.

Acknowledgments

I owe a large debt to Robert Parkinson and Research Press Publishing Company which through its Public Law Division has made my work possible for the past several years. The opportunity to consult with over 100 school programs, other public agencies, and advocacy organizations in about 15 states has given me a broad background against which to assess the needs and the difficulties in implementing laws for the handicapped.

Some remarkable parents have shared with me their struggles in trying to win appropriate services for their children. They have illuminated for me the depth of misunderstanding of the law among many school administrators and the innumerable roadblocks erected to avoid compliance. Thanks Joan, Faye Lynn, Jo Ann, Howard, and Judy.

I have had the privilege of interacting for the past year with the staff of Advocacy, Incorporated, in Austin, Texas— Dayle Bebee, Sandy Adams, Jim Todd, Peter Brooks, and Bill Barbisch. The many hours spent debating issues with them has made me feel much more comfortable about the interpretations advanced in this book.

And finally, I owe a real thanks to Jerry Vlasak of the Bureau of Education for the Handicapped in the U.S. Office of Education. He has patiently answered many questions, explained the rationale behind administrative actions, and worked consistently to move educational agencies toward providing a free, appropriate public education.

1 The Challenge of Change

Legal requirements governing educational services to handicapped children have changed dramatically in the past year. Anyone seeking to implement them must begin with the acceptance of change and the willingness to question assumptions that have governed special education in the past. I have been told recently by several administrators that the provisions of Public Law (Pub. L.) 94-142, the Education for All Handicapped Children Act, are nothing new. They feel that they have been in compliance for years. Such administrators will have difficulty understanding the chaos they will face. Parents, students, and public officials would do well not to rely on such administrators for guidance.

To understand these new requirements, it is helpful to examine those attitudes and practices which must change.

Educational services to handicapped no charity

I recently dealt with the chairman of the board of a private facility which for years had been providing services to mobility impaired children. A parent was complaining about the lack of physical therapy and the official could not understand what right a parent had to complain. It was clear from his approach to the issue that he considered these services to be a gift; and clearly the recipient of a gift is supposed to be grateful for whatever he gets without questioning it.

But educational services to the handicapped are no longer a charitable gift. Basic rights, which will be detailed in later chapters, give an individual opportunities to question service.

1

Parents who have been conditioned to regarding the educational services their children receive as gifts must restructure their thinking. The parent of an 11-year-old physically handicapped girl told me of the 5-year struggle to keep her child in a regular education classroom rather than the segregated classroom where all other handicaps were lumped together and instructed at a lower level. The mother was grateful for what she had achieved—basically her daughter would not be intellectually damaged by a wrongful placement—even though her daughter's physical needs were not being addressed. That mother had grown up in a time when anything done for handicapped children was something extra, and she could not bring herself to make extra demands. That particular school was not meeting the requirements of the law and that parent was joining the school in shortchanging the child.

Educational personnel in private schools, public schools, and other public agencies such as hospitals and mental retardation facilities must also rethink their position. Such professionals may be marvelous people doing wonderful things with difficult children whom others have abandoned. But that does not confer on them any special privileges. I have been told by many educators that they regard themselves as "helping professionals," as the "good guys" whose actions are never questioned. No professional can expect immunity from challenge any longer.

School boards, the communications media, and taxpayers who still think of services to the handicapped as charitable handouts will also have to change. A parent I know recently asked for an impartial due process hearing (see Chapter 8) for her child to demand certain services. The request was brought before a regular school board meeting and a newspaper reporter in attendance wrote an article which suggested that the parent was asking for something outrageous. The parent called the paper and was virtually attacked by the reporter who kept repeating, "Do you expect the school to do everything for your child?" What the parent expected was that the public school meet the child's special educational needs. The reporter simply reflected the public's ignorance about what that means today.

Separate facilities viewed with suspicion

For many years, handicapped children were automatically moved out of programs with the nonhandicapped and into separate facilities. It was thought that this was the best thing that could be done for them. Separate staffs were developed and separate facilities were built and funded. Personnel in these separate facilities were truly interested in the handicapped. They wanted to work with the handicapped and they were trained specifically for the job.

But federal courts began to hear complaints about several problems inherent in separate facilities. First, once a child was identified as handicapped, he got a one-way ticket to a separate facility and would probably never be reintegrated with other nonhandicapped children. Second, even if certain handicapping conditions could be adequately addressed at a separate facility, other problems inevitably arose. Children graduating from these facilities had to enter a world dominated by the nonhandicapped for which they had not been prepared. A lack of social maturity began to be seen as a long-term problem as disabling as other handicaps. So courts began ordering that handicapped children be educated with the nonhandicapped.

We thus have to reorient our thinking about special facilities. They must be viewed with suspicion. They might be newer, cleaner, free of barriers, and have a staff that welcomes the handicapped. But we must now realize that the preferable alternative, for the handicapped and nonhandicapped alike, is the regular facility and the regular program. Only when the nature or severity of the handicap is such that the regular facility cannot be suitable, even after modifications, does the separate facility become an acceptable alternative.

The handicapped in regular education

I was recently asked to address a convention of school principals on current legal issues and indicated that I would stress special education. I was told that the audience would not be receptive because they had to deal with the majority, the nonhandicapped; special education was left to someone else.

For years our schools have maintained separate systems.

Our teacher colleges graduate some people trained for regular education and others for special education. Many regular educational personnel with whom I have worked clearly felt that their sole responsibility to handicapped children was to identify them so they could be moved out of the regular teacher's program.

This all must change now for two reasons: First, any regular educator might be involved in planning a handicapped child's individual education plan (see Chapter 6). Second, once that plan is developed, a regular educator might have the handicapped child in class for all or a portion of a day. The teacher will have to be responsive to the special needs of that child and will have to make appropriate modifications in curriculum and teaching style.

I have been told by some teachers that a handicapped child belongs in their class only if the child can do the work. Therefore these teachers do not do anything different for the handicapped child. In essence, these teachers are trying to show that a handicapped child does not belong in a regular class. I will deal at length with teachers' attitudes in Chapter 6, but it should clearly be stated now that it will no longer be left to regular educational personnel to elect whether to teach the handicapped. When the individual education plan says that the child is ready for a certain type of regular educational placement, and could be successful with a certain type of program, the regular educator must be part of the team responding to that child's constitutional rights.

The federal government and education of the handicapped

Local control of public schools is such a time-honored tradition that many school districts do not welcome the intervention of state educational agencies. And the involvement of the federal government is unthinkable. Most school board officials with whom I have dealt feel they are the sole authority on decisions concerning educational programs.

But most local educational agencies, and virtually all state educational agencies, receive federal funds to help educate the handicapped. To obtain those funds, a plan is submitted to the United States Office of Education (U.S.O.E.). This means local and state practices must be brought into line with the U.S.O.E. regulations. Further, complaints about noncompliance with the approved plan might be brought to the attention of the U.S.O.E. and call for an inquiry from Washington. As will be discussed in Chapter 2, another federal government agency will also be involved, as well as a federally funded advocacy organization. The Department of Health, Education, and Welfare's (H.E.W.) Office for Civil Rights will investigate complaints about local schools and virtually every state now has an independent, federally funded Protection and Advocacy Service to seek compliance with laws affecting the developmentally disabled. Thus, involvement at the federal level is very real.

In some states local schools have been told by their state educational agency not to take this federal scrutiny seriously. They feel that the new federal law is just a carbon copy of the state law that they have been operating under for years so they just keep doing what they have been doing and they believe that they are in compliance. This belief is wrong, even in the few states with laws that come close to the federal requirements.

No local school should be lulled into complacency. The federal government is involved in the education of the handicapped, and this involvement will lead to further changes.

Both public and private facilities affected

Many handicapped children are served in public agencies such as mental retardation facilities. Many others have been placed in private facilities. When such placements occur, the local public school the child might have attended, if nonhandicapped, usually considers the child no longer their responsibility. In fact, some schools feel they are solving their own problem, if not the child's, by placing a child somewhere else and closing the file.

However, as discussed above, any such separate placement (unless the initiation by the parents is completely voluntary) must be viewed as the temporary removal from a regular school program. The public school must continue to be involved in order to determine when they might be able to serve the child again. New federal laws require the public school to have a continuing relationship with the other facility (private or public) by writing and annually revising the child's individual education plan.

While the child is in the private placement or program run by another public agency, the new law requires that the child receive all the protections that the child would receive in the public school. Pertinent information must be shared so that as soon as the services could be appropriately carried out in the public school, the child can be brought back home.

Thus both parties must rethink their relationship. The public school no longer "solves its problem" or terminates its responsibility when it makes a placement elsewhere. Similarly, private placements and facilities run by other branches of government not really controlled by the state education agency must be responsive to the federal laws, remain open to the scrutiny of the enforcement machinery, and work with the local school district.

The "mainstream" and the "least restrictive alternative"

Most schools have long had the rhetoric of placing handicapped children in the "mainstream" (integrated into regular classes with nonhandicapped children). Educational journals for the past decade have been filled with examples of how to do it. But three realities have characterized the practice.

First, most handicapped children were not considered candidates for mainstreaming. Emotionally disturbed children, children with orthopedic impairments, trainable retarded children, children with behavior problems, and children with special health problems were often kept out. Learning disabled children, educable mentally retarded children, and an occasional deaf or blind child whose handicap could be remediated inside the classroom for the purpose of instruction would be considered candidates for mainstreaming.

Second, once the child was mainstreamed, nothing was done for her. The child was considered an acceptable candidate for the regular classroom largely because of how she functioned unaided. If the placement did not work out, the classroom program was not modified—the child was simply removed or often expelled. If the child did remain in the classroom, she might not perform successfully, but would still be maintained there. This is what leads to the perception of many that handicapped children were being "dumped" into the mainstream. The schools collected extra money for including the handicapped but had no extra costs or extra effort.

Third, nonacademic areas were not considered part of the mainstreaming process. The physical education program, extracurricular activities, clubs, and other areas were often considered off limits for the handicapped.

These practices must now change in order to implement the requirements that services be offered in the least restrictive alternative available. All children must be considered candidates for contact with nonhandicapped students during at least a portion of each day. The curriculum and other features of the educational environment must be modified to respond to particular handicapping conditions. And every feature of the public agency program must be opened to the handicapped.

The "least restrictive alternative" (explored in depth in Chapter 7) is a concept that requires a continuum of services to be offered between several agencies. It governs the child's movement in and out of the regular classroom. The "mainstream" is only one end of that continuum. Schools must rethink this concept or they will be wholly unprepared to implement it.

Noneducators judge "appropriateness"

Educational personnel have remained virtually immune to accountability, partly because noneducators have not judged them and partly because no judgment standard had been used. New federal laws, however, call for "appropriate" education. The United States Senate Committee on Labor and Public Welfare discovered when it was examining special education in America that special education was simply something given to a child with no real goal or measurement of progress. Educators have enjoyed the shield employed by many professions: "Don't ask questions. I will tell you whether things are going well."

Chapter 5 will explore the definitions of "appropriate" in depth. Schools must prepare for parents, hearing officers, state reviewing officials, H.E.W. civil rights investigators, and judges to hold up a standard called "appropriate" and make decisions about the schools' educational effort.

Impartial hearing officers

The law has long required impartiality in making administrative decisions. Virtually all schools have traditionally followed a simple model. Complaints are taken up by principals or other administrators and passed up to the superintendent. If they cannot be resolved, there is a hearing before the school board and the losing party can appeal at the state level.

At each step the person hearing the complaint attempts to keep an open mind and that has been considered by schools to be "impartial." But now federal law requires a different procedure for the handicapped. A parent now has recourse to an impartial hearing officer who is not an employee of the school district. The hearing officer's decision can be appealed to the state level (or if the initial hearing were at the state level, it can be appealed into court—more on this in Chapter 7) and the parent does not have to go before local or state school boards.

Predictably, this has infuriated many schools and some states have not, at this writing, worked out all their problems in hearing procedures with the U.S.O.E. Schools must realize that the old way of holding hearings, and the lengthy process involved (in Texas, for example, it took a minimum of 425 days to get from the principal to the state school board) are things of the past.

Parents' role

Special education used to be a game played over the heads of parents. They were not allowed to see most records. They received few notices about their child's program. These notices were usually incomprehensible and often came after the program had already begun or been changed. Their consent was engineered by telling them that if they wanted any service at all for their child they had to consent to the school's recommendations. Parents were seldom invited to staff conferences about the child and evaluations of student progress were not shared with them.

Schools must be ready for a dramatic change. Parents are to be involved in everything. They must be allowed to see any record the school relies upon in programing for the child, to be notified of each step before it is taken, to participate in annual planning and review of progress, and to be able to go to a hearing to challenge anything they dispute.

Possible public backlash

This chapter would not be complete without facing the unpleasant prospect of backlash from the general public. School personnel and parent groups must be willing and able to counter two predictable arguments.

First, parents might feel that schools are doing more for the handicapped than they are for their normal children. Parents of nonhandicapped children have every right to be frustrated about education in today's average school. When they see extra funds being expended, parent conferences, and individual education plans for the handicapped, they will understandably complain.

What must be explained to parents before a backlash builds is that every child is entitled under our Constitution to the offering of an opportunity for education. What is being done for the handicapped is to remove the barriers to that offering. If the child is in a wheelchair, a ramp must be built. The blind need braille texts. The deaf need devices to augment hearing in the classroom or aides to interpret through sign language. The learning disabled need curriculum offered in a different way. The emotionally disturbed need much lower staff-to-student ratios.

Without these bridges to overcome the effect of the handicapping conditions, the handicapped child will not truly be offered an education that he can respond to. It might as well be offered in a foreign language. So what these federal laws seek to do is to bring the handicapped child up to the level where he can sit side by side with the nonhandicapped. They do not intend for the school to do more for the handicapped than for the normal child once the opportunity for education has been made equal.

Undoubtedly the best way to counter this type of backlash

is to offer more parent conferences and begin to develop annual individual goals for the nonhandicapped as well. This will likely be required of all education in the future and will show parents of the nonhandicapped that they have won something from the handicapped students' struggle for equal access to education.

A second predictable complaint, as educational resources are being squeezed for all children, deals with finances. Parents might feel that schools are spending too many tax dollars on the handicapped. Newspapers will undoubtedly report instances of one multiply handicapped child in a program with several adult personnel, or one child placed in a private program with the public school paying several thousand dollars per month. Most handicapped children have mild handicaps which will require little, if any, extra expenditure, but public perception will be different.

School expenditures are only one part of the tax picture. The handicapped child who is not appropriately educated will require tax supported programs the rest of his life; but if properly educated he will save tax dollars. The financial columnist Sylvia Porter (1976) has estimated that it costs $25,000 to rehabilitate a young quadraplegic but that the cost of institutionalization or nursing home care if he were not rehabilitated and lived an average life expectancy would be $750,000 in tax dollars. She has also estimated that "for every $1,000 our nation invests in rehabilitation of the disabled, our economy gets back $9,000—an awesome 9 to 1 return, reflecting the taxes paid by that individual to the federal, state and local government when he gets a job; the halt of social welfare payments when he is able to subsist without this aid; and the funds that flow with multiplying force from this worker as he spends his earned dollars."

School personnel who are statesmanlike can head off backlash and, in fact, get a good public response to the wise investment of our tax dollars in educational services for handicapped children. The most important point is that handicapped children are worth educating. Many parents of nonhandicapped children might mistakenly feel that the educational potential of handicapped children is so low that it is a waste of money. Such a judgment is indefensible.

2 Sources of Law

More than one source of law regulates services to the handicapped. It is not uncommon, however, to find a school administrator relying on just one section of regulations implementing Pub. L. 94-142 and saying that it is "the law."

"The law" is many laws

Detailed in this chapter are the sources of law which regulate services to the handicapped. Service providers should never feel comfortable looking at only one source for an answer; child advocates should not rest until they have investigated all possibly relevant sources of law.

Examining all the sources of law can help one better understand each individual source. School personnel will often point to the word "appropriate" in Pub. L. 94-142 and say it cannot be defined. However, if one looks at the use of that term in all the relevant sources of the law taken together, a definition becomes possible.

Initial exclusion of the handicapped from public schools

The development in the law that produced current federal statutes began nearly a decade ago. At that time many handicapped children were excluded from public school. Little was done about this for two reasons. The first was that the persons being injured were not recognized as having rights that they could complain about. The second was a rigid definition of education.

The categories of clients of services we are concerned with were at the bottom of our legal system: the mentally retarded,

11

the emotionally disturbed, juveniles, and often minority group members. When one of these clients sought to complain about services received from a public agency, the client had three strikes against him: his mental disability, his youth, and the court's natural tendency to side with the administrators.

But in the last decade, federal courts began to require that in dealing with these individuals certain "due process" rights had to be met. The "Due Process Clause" of the Fourteenth Amendment to the United States Constitution requires that when states intervene in citizens' lives they must follow due process before restricting liberty. And courts began to recognize as restrictions of liberty such acts as placing children in institutions or even classifying public school students as retarded.

Initially the procedures required were simply notice and an opportunity for a hearing. Later interpretations of the Due Process Clause expanded its meaning to include notions such as the "least restrictive alternative" (to be discussed in Chapter 7), but the important point to be made here is that it got the clients of these services into court.

The rigid definition of education was the second major reason that the handicapped were initially excluded from public schools. Most states allowed the exclusion of handicapped children if they were deemed incapable of benefiting from a program of public instruction. One reason for this was undoubtedly discriminatory—schools did not want to be bothered with children who were different. A ruling of the Wisconsin Supreme Court (*Beattie v. State Board of Education*) revealed this feeling when it allowed the exclusion of a cerebral palsied child because of his "depressing and nauseating effect on the teachers and school children and . . . [because] he required an undue portion of the teacher's time."

With a concept of education as being the teaching of "normal" subjects to "normal" children, it was very easy for teachers and schools to view time spent with the handicapped as diverting them from their mission. But courts slowly began to recognize what special educators had been insisting on for years—that education was not just the regular academic program. The best statement of this came in a recent case.

Not all children can be educated as we usually think of the term education—grade school, junior high school, et cetera. The diagnosis of Tracy Ann's condition is "psychomotor, growth and developmental retardation with seizure disorder." Such a child required another kind of "education"—how to hold a spoon, feed herself, dress herself, toilet training, et cetera, in addition to speech therapy, psychiatric and psychological treatment, et cetera—all these and more add up to the education of this and other mentally retarded children, and they are entitled to be so educated. (*In the Matter of Tracy Ann Cox*)

Clearly any child could benefit from education under such a standard and state laws which allowed exclusion began to be challenged in federal courts. The challengers often relied on a ruling by the United States Supreme Court in *Brown v. Board of Education:*

Today, education is perhaps the most important function of state and local governments. Compulsory school attendance laws and the great expenditures for education both demonstrate our recognition of the importance of education to our democratic society. It is required in the performance of our most basic public responsibilities, even service in the armed forces. It is the very foundation of good citizenship. Today it is a principal instrument in awakening the child to cultural values, in preparing him for later professional training, and in helping him to adjust normally to his environment. In these days, it is doubtful that any child may reasonably be expected to succeed in life if he is denied the opportunity of an education. Such an opportunity, where the state has undertaken to provide it, is a right which must be made available to all on equal terms.

That basic constitutional assumption—that handicapped children also are entitled to the equal protection of the laws and may not be treated differently without due process of law—was used to successfully challenge the exclusion of the handicapped in two landmark federal cases.

Landmark cases

In Pennsylvania mentally retarded children used to be denied admission to public school programs. On January 7,

1971, the Pennsylvania Association for Retarded Children brought suit in a federal court to declare that practice unconstitutional. In October of that year, a Consent Agreement was entered which established the rights of those retarded children (*Pennsylvania Association for Retarded Children v. Commonwealth of Pennsylvania,* the *P.A.R.C.* case). It won for the retarded not only access to public school programs but also tuition and maintenance costs in approved institutions and homebound instruction where that was appropriate. As the court found in the case:

> Expert testimony in this action indicates that all mentally retarded persons are capable of benefiting from a program of education and training; that the greatest number of retarded persons, given such education and training, are capable of achieving self-sufficiency, and the remaining few, with such education and training, are capable of achieving some degree of self-care; that the earlier such education and training begins, the more thoroughly and the more efficiently a mentally retarded person can benefit at any point in his life and development from a program of education and training.

It was beginning to be unthinkable that handicapped children would simply be denied the benefits of education.

The following month a case was filed in the District of Columbia and judgment was rendered for plaintiffs 10 months later in August of 1972. The practices attacked were broader than those in the *P.A.R.C.* case. They involved all types of handicapped children. And they involved not only the exclusion of the handicapped from services in the beginning, but also the use of suspension and expulsion to eliminate the children whom the school did not want to take the effort to serve. The case was *Mills v. Board of Education.* Judge Waddy of the Federal District Court of the District of Columbia first summed up plaintiffs' allegations:

> [Plaintiffs] allege that although they can profit from an education either in regular classrooms with supportive services or in special classes adapted to their needs, they have been labeled as behavioral problems, mentally retarded, emotionally disturbed or hyperactive, and denied admission to the public schools or ex-

cluded therefrom after admission, with no provision for alternative educational placement or periodic review . . . .

The genesis of this case is found (1) in the failure of the District of Columbia to provide publicly supported education and training to plaintiffs and other "exceptional" children, members of their class, and (2) the excluding, suspending, expelling, reassigning and transferring of "exceptional" children from regular public school classes without affording them due process of law
. . . .

Plaintiffs estimate that there are " . . . 22,000 retarded, emotionally disturbed, blind, deaf, and speech or learning disabled children, and perhaps as many as 18,000 of these children are not being furnished with programs of specialized education . . . ."

[Peter Mills] . . . is twelve years old [and] black . . . . He was excluded from the . . . fourth grade. Peter allegedly was a "behavior problem" and was recommended and approved for exclusion by the principal . . . .

The defendants' conduct here, denying plaintiffs and their class not just an equal publicly supported education but all publicly supported education while providing such education to other children, is a violation of the Due Process Clause.

Not only are plaintiffs and their class denied the publicly supported education to which they are entitled, many are suspended or expelled from regular schooling or specialized instruction or reassigned without any prior hearing and are given no periodic review thereafter. Due process of law requires a hearing prior to exclusion.

A federal standard needed

With the successful conclusions in the *P.A.R.C.* and *Mills* cases, 36 right-to-education cases were soon filed in 27 jurisdictions. The time had clearly come for handicapped children, and the time had come for the federal government to act to declare a clear standard. As the United States Senate Committee on Labor and Public Welfare explained it:

Court action and State laws throughout the nation have made clear that the right to education of handicapped children is a present right, one which is to be implemented immediately. The Committee believes that these State laws and court orders must be implemented and that the Congress of the United States has a responsibility to assure equal protection of the laws and thus to take action to assure that handicapped children throughout the United States have available to them appropriate educational services. (S. Rep. No. 94-168, 1975 U.S. Code Cong. and Ad. News, p. 1441)

The exercise of that Congressional responsibility took two major paths: one involving a nondiscriminatory approach applied to all programs and the other involving the amendment of federal education laws.

On December 9, 1971, Congressman Vanik of Ohio introduced H.R. 12154 (117 Cong. Rec. 45974-75) to amend Title VI of the Civil Rights Act of 1964, 42 U.S.C. 2000-d. That Act prohibited discrimination on the basis of race or national origin in any program receiving federal funds. The Vanik amendment added a prohibition against discrimination based on handicap.

In introducing the bill, Congressman Vanik outlined the plight of the handicapped in America: "In an effort to provide increased assistance and equal opportunity for the handicapped of our Nation, I am today introducing legislation to provide equal treatment of the handicapped in all programs which receive Federal assistance . . . . The masses of the handicapped live and struggle with us, often shunted aside, hidden and ignored. How have we as a nation treated these fellow citizens? . . . Our governments tax these people, their parents and relatives, but fail to provide services for them . . . . The opportunities provided by the Government almost always exclude the handicapped."

On January 20, 1972, a similar measure was introduced in the Senate by Hubert H. Humphrey (S. 3044 at 118 Cong. Rec. 106-07). His remarks made clear that the bill was intended to help handicapped school children: "I introduce . . . a bill . . . to insure equal opportunities for the handicapped by prohibiting needless discrimination in programs receiving federal financial assistance . . . . The time has come when we can no longer tolerate the invisibility of the handicapped in America . . . children who are excluded from school . . . .

"These people have the right to live, to work to the best of their ability—to know the dignity to which every human being is entitled. But too often we keep children whom we regard as 'different' or a 'disturbing influence' out of our schools and community activities altogether, rather than help them develop their abilities in special classes and programs . . . .

"Every child—gifted, normal and handicapped—has a fundamental right to educational opportunity . . . . Justice delayed is justice denied. The Federal Government must now take firm leadership to guarantee the rights of the handicapped, through making needless discrimination illegal in programs receiving federal financial aid."

The Humphrey bill eventually gained 20 cosponsors in the Senate. On March 22, 1972, Senator Humphrey announced additional cosponsors and declared: "This bill responded to an awakening public interest in millions of handicapped children, youth and adults who suffer the profound indignity and despair of isolation, discrimination and maltreatment. It is essential that the rights of these forgotten Americans to equal protection under the laws be effectively enforced" (118 Cong. Rec. 9495).

The Rehabilitation Act of 1973:
Pub. L. 93-112, Section 504

That fall, shortly after the *Mills* decision, the Vanik-Humphrey proposals were added to a bill which became the Rehabilitation Act of 1973, Pub. L. 93-112. When passed a year later, the nondiscrimination proposals became the final section of that Act, Section 504, 29 U.S.C. 794, and provided simply:

> No otherwise qualified handicapped individual in the United States, as defined in section 7(6), shall, solely by reason of his handicap, be excluded from the participation in, be denied the benefits of, or be subjected to discrimination under any program or activity receiving Federal financial assistance.

Both Congressman Vanik and Senator Humphrey recognized Section 504 as solving the problem. Congressman Vanik saw it as "in essence the same as Title VI of the Civil Rights Act of 1964" and observed that it "will soon require that all states provide educational services to all children" [120 Cong. Rec. H 4212-3 (May 21, 1974)].

Senator Humphrey viewed it similarly in remarks shortly after the proposed Rehabilitation Act had been amended: "I am deeply gratified at the inclusion of these provisions, which carry through the intent of original bills which I introduced . . . to amend Title VI and VII of the Civil Rights Act of 1964, to guarantee the right of persons with a mental or physical handicap to participate in programs receiving Federal assistance . . . . The time has come to firmly establish the right of these Americans to dignity and self-respect as equal and contributing members of society, and to end the virtual isolation of millions of children and adults from society" [118 Cong. Rec. S 15947 (Sept. 26, 1972)].

Schools do not respond

But after all this effort there was still a problem. The law was not clear and no school responded. The Rehabilitation Act, before the addition of Section 504, was concerned with employment and programs that would enhance employability. The definition of "handicapped individuals" in the Act seemed limited to employment and therefore Section 504's nondiscrimination language was seen as prohibiting discrimination in employment of the handicapped.

In the 1974 Amendments to the Rehabilitation Act, Congress broadened the definition of "handicapped" and made clear that this included "physically or mentally handicapped children who may be denied admission to federally supported school systems on the basis of their handicap" (S. Rep. No. 93-1297, 1974 U.S. Code. Cong. and Ad. News, pp. 6388-89).

Still there was no response from H.E.W., which would have been expected to promulgate regulations. Without regulations, affected agencies, such as public schools, were not responding.

A group of physically handicapped adults petitioned H.E.W. to issue regulations under the Federal Administrative Procedures Act, 5 U.S.C. 553(e), which allows "an interested person the right to petition for the issuance, amendment, or repeal of a rule." When that seemed to produce no response, James Cherry and the Action League for Physically Handicapped Adults sued H.E.W. Secretary Mathews. The decision in *Cherry v. Mathews* seemed to assure that final regulations would be issued. But a little more drama was required.

Wheelchair sit-ins

When the proposed regulations were issued, a storm of protest arose from public schools and other affected facilities and Secretary Mathews, with only a few months left in office, refused to sign the final regulations. When Secretary Califano took office in January of 1977, he was also reluctant to sign such sweeping regulations. The nondiscrimination sentence in Section 504 had been turned into a rigorous blueprint for affirmative intervention to aid the handicapped. However, after politically embarrassing sit-ins at H.E.W. regional offices, Califano signed the regulations.

The final regulations were published at 42 Fed. Reg. 22676 (May 4, 1977) and are codified as 45 CFR 84. These regulations describe Section 504 as:

> . . . [the] first Federal civil rights law protecting the rights of handicapped persons and reflect[ing] . . . a national commitment to end discrimination on the basis of handicap. The language of Section 504 is almost identical to the comparable nondiscrimination provisions of Title VI of the Civil Rights Act of 1964 and Title IX of the Education Amendments of 1972 (applying to racial discrimination and to discrimination in education on the basis of sex). It establishes a mandate to end discrimination and to bring handicapped persons into the mainstream of American life. The Secretary intends vigorously to implement and enforce that mandate.

Enforcement was to be carried out by H.E.W.'s Office for Civil Rights, but that agency was bottled up in another lawsuit. Under the previous administration, the Office for Civil Rights had developed a large backlog of complaints about discrimination on the basis of race and sex. Organizations concerned about such discrimination sought a judicial order that the backlog of complaints would be processed before any new complaints were investigated. Judge Pratt's decree in *Adams v.*

Califano basically put aside complaints about discrimination on the basis of handicap. Complainants received form letter replies and began to wonder if Section 504 offered any real hope.

H.E.W. told to move

Finally a modification of Judge Pratt's order required H.E.W.'s Office for Civil Rights to move ahead and to vastly increase its field investigation staff. At this writing, investigations are now being scheduled and the full impact of Section 504 will begin to be felt in the school year of 1978-1979. A provision in the Section 504 regulations makes clear that "full compliance" is to be achieved "in no event later than September 1, 1978" [45 CFR 84.33(d)]. Thus, the legislative initiative of Vanik and Humphrey will finally be felt 7 years after it was introduced and 5 years after being passed into law.

The first case to rely on Section 504 states very simply what that law requires.

> The exclusion of a minimally handicapped child from a regular public classroom situation without a bona fide educational reason is in violation of Title V of Public Law 93-112, "The Rehabilitation Act of 1973," 29 U.S.C. 794. The federal statute proscribes discrimination against handicapped individuals in any program receiving federal financial assistance. To deny to a handicapped child access to a regular public school classroom in receipt of federal financial assistance without compelling educational justification constitutes discrimination and a denial of the benefits of such program in violation of the statute. School officials must make every effort to include such children within the regular public classroom situation, even at great expense to the school system. (*Hairston v. Drosick*)

The second educational case to consider Section 504, *Mattie T. v. Holladay,* clearly held that no school program receiving federal funds may deny appropriate educational services to a handicapped child. Many other cases are currently in court.

The Education Amendments of 1974: Pub. L. 93-380

As mentioned above, the Congressional response to the need for a federal standard took two routes: the nondiscrimination approach of Section 504 and the amendment of federal education laws.

In 1966, Congress had created the Bureau of Education for the Handicapped in the Education of the Handicapped Act, Pub. L. 91-230. That Act was expanded in Pub. L. 93-380 which laid the basis for comprehensive planning by the states and protection of handicapped childrens' rights to due process. A summary of the provisions of Pub. L. 93-380 was provided in S. Rep. No. 94-168:

> The Education Amendments of 1974 incorporated the major principles of the right to education cases. That Act added important new provisions to the Education of the Handicapped Act which require the States to: establish a goal of providing full educational opportunities to all handicapped children; provide procedures for insuring that handicapped children and their parents or guardians are guaranteed procedural safeguards in decisions regarding identification, evaluation, and educational placement of handicapped children; establish procedures to insure that, to the maximum extent appropriate, handicapped children, including children in public or private institutions or other care facilities, are educated with children who are not handicapped; and that special classes, separate schooling, or other removal of handicapped children from the regular education environment occurs only when the nature or severity of the handicap is such that education in regular classes with the use of supplementary aids and services cannot be achieved satisfactorily; and, establish procedures to insure that testing and evaluation materials and procedures utilized for the purposes of classification and placement of handicapped children will be selected and administered so as not to be racially or culturally discriminatory.

The Education for
All Handicapped Children Act: Pub. L. 94-142

The most important educational legislation came in 1975. It was originally introduced in the Senate as S. 3614 on May 16, 1972. The Senate Subcommittee on the Handicapped held extensive hearings on its provisions, beginning in April 1973, in New Jersey, Massachusetts, South Carolina, Minnesota, Pennsylvania, and Washington, D.C. The Subcommittee heard over 100 witnesses representing legislators, parents, parent organizations, consumers, education associations, and educators from the local, state, and national level.

S. 3614 was reintroduced in the next session of Congress as S. 6, the Education for All Handicapped Children Act, and passed in 1975 as Pub. L. 94-142.

The job to be done by the public schools was immense. Of the approximately eight million handicapped children requiring special education and related services, the Bureau of Education for the Handicapped estimated that only half were receiving an appropriate education. Almost two million handicapped children received no educational services at all and over two million received an inappropriate education. [Figures are from S. Rep. No. 94-168 which accompanied S. 6 when it was reported out of committee; they are also contained in Pub. L. 94-142 3(b), 20 U.S.C. 1401(b).]

The Senate Committee noted in reporting out S. 6 that not correcting this situation would cause an enormous expense of tax dollars as well as lost opportunities for the handicapped. The Committee found that families were forced to find services at great distance from their homes and at great expense. Sometimes, out of desperation, families that become strapped financially and emotionally by trying to find services needlessly placed children into institutions which cost billions of dollars merely "to maintain persons in . . . sub-human conditions" (S. Rep. No. 94-168). The uneducated handicapped then remain tax burdens for the rest of their lives when they might have become taxpayers.

Thus schools were charged to include all handicapped schoolage children in appropriate programs of public education. Schools were given a full 2 years, from the enactment of Pub. L. 94-142 in the fall of 1975 to October of 1977, to get ready for the Act's requirements. Many schools did not use the time wisely and missed the opportunity to assess needs, develop resources, and train staff.

Regulations implementing Pub. L. 94-142 were published at 42 Fed. Reg. 42474 (August 23, 1977), and codified at 45 CFR 121a. Similar to Section 504, they require full compliance with the requirement of a "free appropriate public education" by "not later than September 1, 1978."

The Developmentally Disabled Assistance and Bill of Rights Act: Pub. L. 94-103

While these changes were occurring in regard to all handicapped citizens, some equally important changes were taking place in regard to the provision of services to those handicapped persons who are classified as "developmentally disabled" (mentally retarded, autistic, cerebral palsied, or epileptic individuals). Many developmentally disabled individuals faced institutionalization. During the period from 1971 to 1977 federal courts began to recognize that many of these citizens were inappropriately placed in residential institutions and, once there, nothing was done that would return them to a more normal setting.

So the Developmentally Disabled Assistance Act was amended in 1975 to include a "Bill of Rights" section. As stated in the proposed regulations [at 41 Fed. Reg. 36581-82 (Aug. 30, 1976)], one purpose of that Act was to specify the rights of the developmentally disabled:

> . . . [t]hat developmentally disabled persons have the right to appropriate treatment, services, and habilitation; that programs should be designed to maximize the developmental potential of the person; and that the Federal Government and States have an obligation to assure that public funds are not provided in programs which do not deliver appropriate treatment, services, and habilitation or do not meet appropriate minimum standards as specified in the Act.

Pub. L. 94-103, the Developmentally Disabled Assistance and Bill of Rights Act, had final regulations published at 42 Fed. Reg. 5277 (Jan. 27, 1977), and is codified at 45 CFR 1385-86. It places certain requirements on state departments to assure appropriateness of placement, to provide interaction between residential and community facilities, and to provide for the educational needs of handicapped residents.

Thus, the sources of law supporting full services for the handicapped are growing. In addition to the many court cases, there are four federal statutes and their implementing regulations. One additional source needs to be mentioned.

State's responsibility

Pub. L. 94-142 requires at 45 CFR 121a.110-284 that each state education agency must annually submit a program to explain how the law's requirements will be met. That plan must be approved by the Bureau of Education for the Handicapped before the next year's funding is sent to the state.

The state education agency's plan must be developed in consultation with the public. The public, particularly the handicapped and specially interested persons, must be notified of the proposed plan. There must be at least 30 days for interested persons to make written comments about the proposed plan. The state education agency must also hold public hearings on the proposed plan at times and places that afford the public an opportunity to participate. Before adopting the final plan, the state educational agency must review the public's written and oral comments and make any necessary modifications.

When the state plan is sent to Washington, it must be accompanied by assurances that state laws and local policies are consistent with Pub. L. 94-142. There must also be a signed assurance that the plan complies with nondiscrimination requirements of Section 504.

These assurances have been held by courts to create an additional source of law. The annual program plan is no longer a statement of philosophy or vague goals. It is a solemn promise by the officials of the state education agency that they will abide by the plan as written. Thus, persons who will be affected—education personnel, parents, handicapped children, representatives and organizations of the handicapped, and taxpayers—should use the public comment period to assure that what is required by Pub. L. 94-142 is indeed in the state plan. Once that plan is sent to Washington and approved by the Bureau of Education for the Handicapped, it becomes part of the law.

The handicapped become "third-party beneficiaries" of the state plan. The two main parties, the state education agency and the Bureau of Education for the Handicapped, have agreed to do certain things in order to benefit a third party, the handicapped. Courts have held that such third-party beneficiaries can sue to enforce the provisions of a plan, so plans do become an important new source of legal regulation. [See *Lemon v. Bossier Parish.* Also see 42 Fed. Reg. 29552 (July 16, 1976).]

Enforcement of the law

Enforcement of these laws will come from two important agencies already mentioned. The Bureau of Education for the Handicapped will assess state plans submitted to it and audit compliance with these plans. Those audits, to occur biannually in each state, will include input from the handicapped and visits to local school districts. The Office for Civil Rights in H.E.W. will respond to complaints about discrimination on the basis of a handicap. They will pursue individual investigations, or, where the complaints are numerous and suggest a pattern or practice of discrimination, they may initiate a system-wide investigation.

One additional quasi-public group will be vital in enforcement of these new laws. Pub. L. 94-103 creates in each state an organization for the protection and advocacy of individual rights. The regulations provide that not later than October 1, 1977:

> (1) the State will have in effect a system to protect and advocate the rights of persons with developmental disabilities, (2) such system will have the authority to pursue legal, administrative, and other appropriate remedies to insure the protection of the rights of such persons who are receiving treatment, services or habilitation within the State, and (3) such system will be independent of any State agency which provides treatment, services or habilitation to persons with developmental disabilities. (45 CFR 1386.70)

Each state's Protection and Advocacy Service is limited to pursuing issues involving the developmentally disabled, but the remedies they achieve will establish precedents for all handicapped children. Thus, the legal and administrative actions they take will add another element to the large number of sources of law to which every educational agency must respond.

3 Eligible Children: An Affirmative Responsibility

Identifying and assessing handicapped children who have a right to special education and related services is a serious responsibility of the schools. Upon discovering the number of children either receiving no services or inappropriate services, Congress mandated a nationwide effort generally known as "Child Find." It required each state to insure that "[a]ll children who are handicapped, regardless of the severity of their handicap, and who are in need of special education and related services are identified, located and evaluated." That includes "children in all public and private agencies and institutions in the State" as well as those totally unserved. (See 45 CFR 121a.128 and Comment.)

Assessment easily corrupted

The history of special education assessment must make us cautious as to how this responsibility is discharged. Several analyses indicate that assessment practices are easily corrupted to serve the convenience of the school system rather than the child. (See Task Force on Children Out of School, 1971, and Weatherly & Lipsky, 1977, p. 171.)

These studies indicated several typical school assessment practices. Many children who might have met eligibility criteria simply were not assessed because assessment takes time, money, and effort. Troublesome students whom the teachers would like to be rid of were quickly processed and, in some cases, test scores were rigged so that disruptive students could be excluded from regular classes. Normal children were often misclassified as retarded because of a bias in testing instruments. Where screening procedures relied heavily on one type of specialty, the disorders identified were directly related to that specialty. "For example, System B, which relied much more heavily on speech specialists to conduct screening than the other two systems, referred more than twice as many children for evaluations because of speech problems. In many instances, those doing the screening were actually referring children to themselves. That is, the speech specialist conducting screening would more than likely participate in the core evaluation and eventually treat the child. This overlap of functions suggests that the local systems need to guard not only against failing to identify children in need of special services, but also against unnecessarily recruiting children not in need of special services" (Weatherly & Lipsky, 1977, p. 184).

Administrators sometimes gave instructions to cut back on evaluations because of the cost of the services that might be involved if the child was found to be eligible. The pattern that emerges is a biasing of the "scheduling of assessments in favor of children who were behavior problems, who were not likely to cost the system money, or who met the needs of school personnel seeking to practice their individual specialties" (Weatherly & Lipsky, 1977, p. 194).

Student's right to be in mainstream

School personnel must realize how serious the proper functioning of the assessment process is. Students have a right to be in the educational mainstream where they can enjoy access to an opportunity for education equal with everyone else (*Brown v. Board of Education*) unless the school has a legitimate interest in treating them differently. If the referral for evaluation is wrongly motivated or if the assessment is flawed, then the mistake is one of constitutional dimensions.

The Due Process Clause of the Fourteenth Amendment to the Constitution requires certain protections before students' protected interests are affected. One of those interests, recognized by the United States Supreme Court in *Goss v. Lopez,* is "a student's legitimate entitlement to a public education as a property interest which is protected by the Due Process Clause and which may not be taken away . . . without adherence to the minimum procedures required by that Clause." The Court recognized as a deprivation anything that "could seriously damage the students' standing with their fellow pupils and their teachers as well as interfere with later opportunities for higher education and employment." The Court noted a listing by the lower court, whose decision they affirmed (*Lopez v. Williams*), of "psychological harm to the student" when certain things are done to a student which are "a blow to the student's self-esteem," which make the student "feel powerless and helpless," or which cause the student to be "stigmatized by his teachers and school administrators as a deviant." That court noted the consequences of the family or neighbor's branding the student as different.

Certainly any school must recognize that wrongful classification would be a stigmatization, would psychologically harm the student, would lessen the chances for future education and employment, and would change the student in the eyes of teachers, peers, and family. More care must certainly be taken by schools than they have exercised in the past.

School's duty of referral

On the other hand, schools must not fail to refer legitimately suspected students in an attempt to avoid the problems listed above. A school's failure of referral can be just as wrong as the expedient assessment of a handicap, as indicated in the case of *Pierce v. Board of Education:*

> From 1971 to February, 1974 the plaintiff attended the F. W. Riley School in the City of Chicago. During that time the minor-plaintiff was discovered to be suffering from a specific learning disability. . . . [T]he defendant was advised of this fact by the minor-plaintiff's parents and various of the plaintiff's privately retained physicians, who recommended that the boy be transferred from the regular or normal classes of instruction to classes known as special education classes or learning disability classes. Nevertheless, the defendant failed and refused to either transfer the minor to these classes or undertake their own testing and

evaluation of the boy. As a result of the defendant's failure to comply with their statutory duties, the plaintiff remained in regular classes at the F. W. Riley School from 1971 to 1974, where he was required to compete with students not suffering from a learning disability and as a result sustained severe and permanent emotional and psychic injury requiring hospitalization and medical treatment.

The Illinois Appellate Court found that the school does have a duty to identify those in need of special services. Doing nothing, the Court said, would be an intentional breach of the school board's duty and could make school board members liable for any damages shown.

The key: Eligibility criteria

What can schools use as a road map to find their way between the wrongful deprivation of constitutionally protected interests and the failure to meet the affirmative standard for identification of Pub. L. 94-142? The key is obviously the eligibility criteria. Each state must have spelled out in their annual program plan their procedures for identification and evaluation. Every local school district or other public agency that performs assessments must have guidelines that control the eligibility criteria and evaluation procedures.

At a minimum, the guidelines must include the definitions of handicapping conditions found in the federal law at 45 CFR 121a.5:

(a) As used in this part, the term "handicapped children" means those children evaluated in accordance with sections 121a.530-534 as being mentally retarded, hard of hearing, deaf, speech impaired, visually handicapped, seriously emotionally disturbed, orthopedically impaired, other health impaired, deaf-blind, multihandicapped, or as having special learning disabilities, who because of those impairments need special education and related services.

(b) The terms used in this definition are defined as follows:

(1) "Deaf" means a hearing impairment which is so severe that the child is impaired in processing linguistic information through hearing, with or without amplification, which adversely affects education.

(2) "Deaf-blind" means concomitant hearing and visual impairments, the combination of which causes such severe communication and other developmental and educational problems that they cannot be accommodated in special education programs solely for deaf or blind children.

(3) "Hard of hearing" means a hearing impairment, whether permanent or fluctuating, which adversely affects a child's educational performance but which is not included under the definition of "deaf" in this section.

(4) "Mentally retarded" means significantly subaverage general intellectual functioning existing concurrently with deficits in adaptive behavior and manifested during the developmental period, which adversely affects a child's educational performance.

(5) "Multihandicapped" means concomitant impairments (such as mentally retarded-blind, mentally retarded-orthopedically impaired, etc.) the combination of which causes such severe educational problems that they cannot be accommodated in special education programs solely for one of the impairments. The term does not include deaf-blind children.

(6) "Orthopedically impaired" means a severe orthopedic impairment which adversely affects a child's educational performance. The term includes impairments caused by congenital anomaly (e.g., clubfoot, absence of some member, etc.), impairments caused by disease (e.g., poliomyelitis, bone tuberculosis, etc.), and impairments from other causes (e.g., cerebral palsy, amputations, and fractures or burns which cause contractures).

(7) "Other health impaired" means limited strength, vitality, or alertness, due to chronic or acute health problems such as heart condition, tuberculosis, rheumatic fever, nephritis, asthma, sickle cell anemia, hemophilia, epilepsy, lead poisoning, leukemia, or diabetes, which adversely affects a child's educational performance.

(8) "Seriously emotionally disturbed" is defined as follows:

(i) The term means a condition exhibiting one or more of the following characteristics over a long period of time and to a marked degree, which adversely affects educational performance.

(A) An inability to learn which cannot be explained by intellectual, sensory, or health factors;

(B) An inability to build or maintain satisfactory interpersonal relationships with peers and teachers;

(C) Inappropriate types of behavior or feelings under normal circumstances;

(D) A general pervasive mood of unhappiness or depression; or

(E) A tendency to develop physical symptoms or fears associated with personal or school problems.

(ii) The term includes children who are schizophrenic or autistic. The term does not include children who are socially maladjusted, unless it is determined that they are seriously emotionally disturbed.

(9) "Specific learning disability" means a disorder in one or more of the basic psychological processes involved in understanding or in using language, spoken or written, which may manifest itself in an imperfect ability to listen, think, speak, read, write, spell, or to do mathematical calculations. The term includes such conditions as perceptual handicaps, brain injury, minimal brain dysfunction, dyslexia, and developmental aphasia. The term does not include children who have learning problems which are primarily the result of visual, hearing, or motor handicaps, of mental retardation, of emotional disturbance, or of environmental, cultural, or economic disadvantage.

(10) "Speech impaired" means a communication disorder, such as stuttering, impaired articulation, a language impairment, or a voice impairment, which adversely affects a child's educational performance.

(11) "Visually handicapped" means a visual impairment which, even with correction, adversely affects a child's educational performance. The term includes both partially seeing and blind children.

Problem definitions

Three federal definitions—"mentally retarded," "seriously emotionally disturbed," and "specific learning disability"—are very loose and assessment in these areas is problematic.

"Mental retardation" can no longer be assessed by one individual using one criterion. It must include not only the Intelligence Quotient (I.Q.), but also assessment of deficits in adaptive behavior. There is disagreement among experts about the ease of using adaptive behavior scales (see Coulter & Morrow, 1977). One can expect constant complaints that a child in the regular classroom is really "educable," that a child treated as "educable" is really "trainable," and vice versa. The important thing is that the evaluation do more than just hang a label on the child—it is not an evaluation until it produces a prescription. With that prescription the school will know where the child needs to be served and can avoid needless battles over "educable/trainable."

The definition of "seriously emotionally disturbed" includes subjective value-laden words such as "marked degree," "satisfactorily," "inappropriate," "normal," and "unhappiness." Definitions which allow such subjectivity will mean that school personnel who employ them will be open to charges that they were simply trying to get rid of a troublesome student. To the degree that each of these terms can be operationally defined so that different individuals could agree that the "disturbed" behavior is in fact exhibited by the child, there would be fewer challenges.

"Learning disability" was so difficult to define by the Congress that, even though they had been using the term for several years in federal laws, they required the Commissioner of Education to define it. That definition is published at 42 Fed. Reg. 65081 (Dec. 29, 1977). It follows the same substantive explanation as the definition of specific learning disability printed above, but adds procedures for a multidisciplinary evaluation team which must observe the child in action. One individual, looking at one piece of information and never having had direct contact with the child, can no longer make a determination that a child is "learning disabled."

Section 504 defines "handicapped" at 45 CFR 84.3(j) very broadly. Any person is eligible who has a physical or mental impairment which substantially limits one or more major life activities such as caring for one's self, performing manual tasks, and learning. This definition is not intended to give schools a precise tool to work with but simply indicates the scope of coverage of Section 504.

School's affirmative duty to locate children

Once eligibility criteria are in place, schools have the affirmative duty to locate all children who might fit the criteria. That includes children who have never been served, children currently in school but never diagnosed as in need of special education, children in other public agencies and institutions, and even children in private schools. (See 45 CFR 121a.220 and Comment.)

The local education agency (L.E.A.) has the responsibility for children in its jurisdiction. That obviously includes children in the L.E.A. operated programs. It also includes children placed by the L.E.A. in programs operated by other agencies but still in the L.E.A.'s jurisdiction, and children placed by other agencies in programs in the L.E.A. jurisdiction. This eliminates a federal problem. If every L.E.A. does its job, all eligible children will be identified, but if L.E.A.'s are allowed to argue over who is responsible for locating and placing children, then many children must wait to be served.

Some schools still try to evade their responsibility and argue that it is really up to the parents to press for service. Some school officials argue that if a parent doesn't fight for special education, it's not the school's responsibility. In *Frederick L. v. Thomas* the federal court reviewed how unfair it would be to place this burden on the parent:

> It is disputed whether parent referrals through parent-initiated due process hearings are an effective method for identifying LD's. There is not enough experience with the due process procedures to make definitive findings on this question. To utilize the procedure the parent has to (a) recognize her child is not functioning academically, (b) recognize that the cause of the child's underachievement may be something that requires special education instruction, (c) know that due process hearings are available, (d) believe that through a due process hearing her child—though not a severe behavior problem—may receive special help, (e) properly carry out the procedures for initiating the hearing which includes obtaining an expert psychiatric opinion.

Obviously the duty rests with the service provider to identify children in need of services.

The necessity of identification

Some schools maintain that if children are receiving some service, if they are in the regular classroom, then "identification" is not needed because services are already being provided.

That argument was flatly rejected in *Frederick L. v. Thomas.*

> There is ample expert testimony in the record to support the conclusion that some learning disabled students would be afforded appropriate educational opportunities if they were placed in regular classes with "supporting services" consisting of instruction in remedial programs not designated special education. For that matter, appropriate supporting services for some LD's may be nothing more than monitoring their academic performance in regular classrooms so that new learning problems that arise because of their disabilities do not go undetected. Placing exceptional children in regular classes in this manner is called "mainstreaming." Under the regulations, it is a preferred strategy.
>
> We cannot find, however, that learning disabled students whose disabilities have *not* been identified and who are in regular classes, or in general remedial programs, or some combination of the two, are properly "mainstreamed" .... There must first be a diagnosis of the child's exceptionality, and then a determination that mainstreaming under prescribed conditions will be an appropriate placement.

The child must be identified, evaluated, and properly placed, even if placement is back to the child's original classes.

Obviously nothing less than a vigorous effort will meet Congressional intent. The recent case of *Mattie T. v. Holladay* found that Mississippi was not attempting to identify all eligible students. As explained in the plaintiff's motion for summary judgment:

> Parents in six school districts located throughout the state whose children are in desperate need of an education have had their children excluded from school entirely or denied an appropriate education ....
>
> The Senate Committee on Labor and Public Welfare explained the need for an identification program as follows:
>
> At present, *failure to identify handicapped children represents a major barrier to fulfillment of state programs.* For example, New Jersey law provides that local education agencies must offer special programs to handicapped children, but the lack of identification programs is a major factor in keeping the percentage of the children served at less than the 50% level.
>
> The committee is convinced that a more intense effort must be

expended in the identification of handicapped children. Parents testifying at . . . hearings, whether or not they had been successful in locating services for their children, were unanimous in their view that they had almost always been left to themselves to find needed services for their children. In this regard, most of these parents were able to find services or able to have their children properly identified as handicapped only as a result of great individual efforts on their own behalf.

A full assessment

Once children are identified as potentially eligible, an equally serious responsibility must be discharged by the agency. Children must be assessed fully. A full and fair assessment requires examination into every area "related to the suspected disability, including, where appropriate, health, vision, hearing, social and emotional status, general intelligence, academic performance, communicative status, and motor abilities" [45 CFR 121a.532(f)]. This would truly require a multidisciplinary team. To assess each of these areas might require a physician, optometrist, audiologist, social worker, psychologist, teacher, speech therapist, physical therapist, or occupational therapist.

The burden is, of course, on the L.E.A. to see that the needed diagnoses are made at no expense to the parent. Further, the L.E.A. must make arrangements for the needed assessments. Schools can no longer give parents a list of specialists and tell them to get the tests done at their own expense. Pub. L. 94-142's legislative history, the regulations, and the developing body of federal judicial decisions are clear on that.

A nondiscriminatory assessment

A common problem in assessment involves the use of tests which discriminate against children on the basis of race, culture, or sensory disability. As a result of these tests children are wrongly classified. A typical abuse is I.Q. testing which shows mental retardation only because of racial bias (see *Larry P. v. Riles*) or because the student being tested spoke another primary language (see *Diana v. State Board of Education*).

This practice still occurs, as revealed in the recent case of

Mattie T. v. Holladay. The plaintiff's memorandum in that case, and the affidavits of expert witnesses, explain the concern over misclassification:

> In enacting Section 613(a)(13)(C), Congress recognized that a great many poor and minority children were being mistakenly classified as mentally retarded on the basis of racially and culturally biased intelligence tests.
>
> Congress was concerned that minority children who are misclassified as mentally retarded would suffer the social stigma of being called retarded, be inappropriately placed in segregated classes for mentally retarded children and denied contacts with nonhandicapped children, and receive substantially limited curriculum opportunities.
>
> The affidavit of Dr. Jane R. Mercer . . . provides an extensive analysis of the problem of misclassification and identifies four major consequences of being labeled mentally retarded:
>
> First, these children are usually placed in programs separated from "nonhandicapped" children and isolated from the mainstream of school life. This denies them the benefit of participating in regular school activities, learning from their peers and developing the independence that comes from growing up in a normal environment with children the same age who have a range of abilities and behavior. The denial of a normal environment and of challenging role models is especially damaging to these children's development.
>
> Second, there is a terrible stigma to being labeled mentally retarded. Parents reported that their children were ashamed to be seen entering the "MR" room because they were often teased by other children about being "MR's." These children would feign illness in order to remain out of school so as not to be seen entering the "MR" class.
>
> Third, the curriculum in the classes in which these children were placed is generally so limited that many children rapidly become educationally retarded, relative to children the same age who remain in the regular program . . . . Teachers expected less in the way of academic performance from the children in these classes. They, therefore, made fewer demands on them and presented less information. As a consequence, of course, the children then did fail to achieve at a normal rate, and the teachers' original lower expectations thus become a self-fulfilling prophecy.

And fourth, these children tend to be placed permanently in classes for the mentally retarded. Our study showed that only one child in five is *ever* returned to the regular class.

In his affidavit Dr. Milton Budoff . . . describes the "harmful and inhumane effects" of the practice of isolating children who are labeled mentally retarded from other children and states:

Of course, to the extent children are being misclassified mentally retarded, their placement into separate special classes will be utterly devastating to their academic and social development.

Numerous education experts, psychologists and parents testified that the practice of classifying children as mentally retarded based primarily on scores on intelligence, aptitude or achievement tests (i.e., I.Q. tests), not only is bad educational practice, but results in serious over-classification of blacks and other minority children.

Congress recognized the problems with discriminatory testing in S. Rep. No. 94-168:

The Committee is alarmed about the abuses which occur in the testing and evaluation of children, and is concerned that expertise in the proper use of testing and evaluation procedures falls short of the prolific use and development of testing and evaluation tools. The usefulness and mechanistic ease of testing should not become so paramount in the educational process that the negative effects of such testing are overlooked . . . .

. . . Regulations should assure that: (1) tests and other materials used for placement have been properly and professionally evaluated for the specific purpose for which they are being used; (2) no single test or type of test or procedure is used as the sole criterion for placement and that all relevant information with regard to the functional abilities of the child is utilized in the placement determination; and (3) tests and other evaluation procedures include assessment of specific areas of educational need so that provision of special education and related services can be limited to areas directly related to the child's need, so that broad and unspecific classifications of handicapping do not occur. In particular, such regulations should assure that test selection and administration provide absolute protection that a test administered to a student with a sensory, motor, speech, hearing, visual, or other communicative disability, or to a student who is bilingual, accurately reflects the child's ability in the area tested and not the child's impaired communication skill or the fact that the child is not skilled in English.

These requirements have now become part of the law. The regulations implementing Pub. L. 94-142 are reproduced below and are identical to Section 504's regulations at 45 CFR 84.35(a)-(c).

45 CFR 121a.531   Preplacement evaluation.

Before any action is taken with respect to the initial placement of a handicapped child in a special education program, a full and individual evaluation of the child's educational needs must be conducted in accordance with the requirements of section 121a.532.

45 CFR 121a.532   Evaluation procedures.

State and local educational agencies shall insure, at a minimum, that:

(a) Tests and other evaluation materials:

(1) Are provided and administered in the child's native language or other mode of communication, unless it is clearly not feasible to do so;

(2) Have been validated for the specific purpose for which they are used; and

(3) Are administered by trained personnel in conformance with the instructions provided by their producer;

(b) Tests and other evaluation materials include those tailored to assess specific areas of educational need and not merely those which are designed to provide a single general intelligence quotient;

(c) Tests are selected and administered so as best to ensure that when a test is administered to a child with impaired sensory, manual, or speaking skills, the test results accurately reflect the child's aptitude or achievement level or whatever other factors the test purports to measure, rather than reflecting the child's impaired sensory, manual, or speaking skills (except where those are the factors which the test purports to measure);

(d) No single procedure is used as the sole criterion for determining an appropriate educational program for a child; and

(e) The evaluation is made by a multidisciplinary team or group of persons, including at least one teacher or other specialist with knowledge in the area of suspected disability.

(f) The child is assessed in all areas related to the suspected disability, including, where appropriate, health, vision, hearing, social and emotional status, general intelligence, academic performance, communicative status, and motor abilities.

Comment. Children who have a speech impairment as their primary handicap may not need a complete battery of assessments (e.g., psychological, physical, or adaptive behavior). However, a qualified speech-language pathologist would (1) evaluate each speech impaired child using procedures that are appropriate for the diagnosis and appraisal of speech and language disorders, and (2) where necessary, make referrals for additional assessments needed to make an appropriate placement decision.

45 CFR 121a.533   Placement procedures.

(a) In interpreting evaluation data and in making placement decisions, each public agency shall:

(1) Draw upon information from a variety of sources, including aptitude and achievement tests, teacher recommendations, physical condition, social or cultural background, and adaptive behavior;

(2) Insure that the placement decision is made by a group of persons, including persons knowledgeable about the child, the meaning of the evaluation data, and the placement options.

Using the assessment data

Once the multidisciplinary team has all the assessment data in-house there should be a review before decisions are made. A helpful instrument has been developed by Region One Education Service Center, Edinburg, Texas, to judge the usability of assessment data (Masters & Hylander, 1977). The following checklist is used, with each criterion having to be met to the review committee's satisfaction.

- Report is written in understandable language.
- Tools or processes used in evaluation are identified.
- Setting in which evaluation occurred is described.
- Evaluation contains concise statement of specific results.
- Identification of problem areas identified by evaluation.
- Identification of problem areas identified by behavioral observation.
- Evaluation contains concise statement of strengths

and weaknesses.
- Information is relevant to educational planning.
- Information describes conditions which influence ability to perform tasks.

An inability to satisfactorily meet any of the above criteria would leave the evaluation team susceptible to later challenge. Diagnostic generalities and labels without prescriptions will not meet the constitutional standard.

The right to independent evaluation

Pub. L. 94-142 clearly recognizes that some schools might refuse to test, might test inadequately, or might make mistakes. To provide a safeguard against this, parents have a right to an independent education evaluation.

Previously, if a parent was dissatisfied, sought an independent diagnosis, and took it to the school, schools would typically not respond, treating the outside diagnosis as predictably biased in the parents' favor. But now a school must respond to an independent diagnosis, must keep it in the record folder, and it "must be considered by the public agency in any decision made with respect to the provision of a free appropriate public education to the child" [45 CFR 121a.503(c) (1)].

Further, if the school evaluation, with which the parent was dissatisfied, is not "appropriate," then the school must reimburse the parent for the cost of the independent evaluation. That question of "appropriateness" is to be determined in an impartial due process hearing (to be discussed in Chapter 8).

There are several steps involved in the process. First, the parents have a right to be informed of their right to an independent educational evaluation. If they are dissatisfied with the school's evaluation, the parents should alert the school that they are dissatisfied, do not consider it appropriate, and are considering an outside evaluation. The school then might make any of four responses: (1) it might decide that what it is doing is appropriate and call for an impartial hearing to sustain that judgment; (2) it might order an outside evaluation on its own; (3) it might inform the parents where they could get such an evaluation at no cost; or (4) it might tell the parents the criteria under which the independent evaluation must be obtained, including the location of the evaluation and the qualifications of the examiner, so the parents' evaluation will be reimbursable.

Assuming that the parents seek an independent evaluation, they must then procure the evaluation from someone who is not an employee of the public agency responsible for the child in question but who meets the school's criteria. The parent sends the bill for the evaluation to the school and the school must either pay the bill or call for an impartial due process hearing to prove that the school's evaluation was "appropriate." The school must shoulder the burden of proof at the hearing. If the hearing officer is dissatisfied with both evaluations, he can order further evaluation at public expense. If the parents lose, they do not get reimbursed. In any case, the school must incorporate the independent evaluation into the child's record and use it in future educational decision making.

Regulations governing independent evaluations

The specific regulations governing the independent evaluation procedure are at 45 CFR 121a.503:

(a) *General.* (1) The parents of a handicapped child have the right under this part to obtain an independent educational evaluation of the child, subject to paragraphs (b) through (e) of this section.

(2) Each public agency shall provide to parents, on request, information about where an independent educational evaluation may be obtained.

(3) For the purposes of this part:

(i) "Independent educational evaluation" means an evaluation conducted by a qualified examiner who is not employed by the public agency responsible for the education of the child in question.

(ii) "Public expense" means that the public agency either pays for the full cost of the evaluation or insures that the evaluation is otherwise provided at no cost to the parent, consistent with section 121a.301 of Subpart C.

(b) *Parent right to evaluation at public expense.* A parent has the right to an independent educational evaluation at public expense if the parent disagrees with an evaluation obtained by the public agency. However, the public agency may initiate a hearing under section 121a.506 of this subpart to show that its evaluation is appropriate. If the final decision is that the evaluation is appropriate, the parent still has the right to an independent educational evaluation, but not at public expense.

(c) *Parent initiated evaluations.* If the parent obtains an independent educational evaluation at private expense, the results of the evaluation:

(1) Must be considered by the public agency in any decision made with respect to the provision of a free appropriate public education to the child and

(2) May be presented as evidence at a hearing under this subpart regarding that child.

(d) *Requests for evaluations by hearing officers.* If a hearing officer requests an independent educational evaluation be obtained, the criteria under which the evaluation is obtained, including the location of the evaluation and the qualifications of the examiner, must be the same as the criteria which the public agency uses when it initiates an evaluation.

4 A "Free" Public Education

Once a child has been evaluated and it is determined that the child needs special education, a free, appropriate public education must be provided. (See Chapter 5 for a discussion of an "appropriate" education.)

"Free" defined

"Free" indicates that education is provided without charge to the parents. The recognition of the right to education at no cost to the parent has been developing in the courts since *P.A.R.C.* and *Mills.* Two of the most eloquent statements of this equitable right of parents came in New York cases:

> It would be a denial of the right of equal protection and morally inequitable not to reimburse the parents of a handicapped child for monies they have advanced in order that their child may attend a private school for the handicapped when no public facilities were available while other children who are more fortunate can attend public school without paying tuition and without regard to the assets and income of their parents. (*In Re K*)

> [T]o order a parent to contribute to the education of his handicapped child when free education is supplied to all other children would be a denial of the constitutional right of equal protection. (*In Re Downey*)

That right is now firmly stated in both Pub. L. 94-142 and in the regulations implementing it and Section 504. Schools still make, however, any of six arguments which have served them

well in the past in getting parents to pay for their child's special
education. These arguments are examined below so that schools
will stop using them and parents will be able to challenge them.

Argument 1: "Schools cannot afford it."

Many school districts claim they just cannot meet the man-
date because of a lack of funds. It seems clear to them that if
they do not have the resources, they should not have to offer
the services. But lack of funds is no excuse under either Pub. L.
94-142 or Section 504. Both Acts rely heavily on the federal
court's response in *Mills* when the school board said that they
could not afford to educate all handicapped children:

> The defendants are required by the Constitution of the United
> States, the District of Columbia Code, and their own regulations
> to provide a publicly-supported education for these "excep-
> tional" children. Their failure to fulfill this clear duty to include
> and retain these children in the public school system, or other-
> wise provide them with publicly-supported education, and their
> failure to afford them due process hearing and periodic review,
> cannot be excused by the claim that there are insufficient funds.
> In *Goldberg v. Kelley*, . . . the Supreme Court, in a case that
> involved the right of a welfare recipient to a hearing before termi-
> nation of his benefits, held that Constitutional rights must be
> afforded citizens despite the greater expense involved. The Court
> stated . . . that "the State's interests that his [the welfare recip-
> ient's] payments not be erroneously terminated, clearly out-
> weighs the State's competing concern to prevent any increase in
> its fiscal and administrative burdens." Similarly the District of
> Columbia's interest in educating the excluded children must clear-
> ly outweigh its interest in preserving its financial resources. If
> sufficient funds are not available to finance all of the services and
> programs that are needed and desirable in the system then the
> available funds must be expended equitably in such a manner that
> no child is entirely excluded from a publicly-supported education
> consistent with his needs and ability to benefit therefrom. The
> inadequacies of the District of Columbia Public School System,
> whether occasioned by insufficient funding or administrative
> inefficiency, certainly cannot be permitted to bear more heavily
> on the "exceptional" or handicapped child than on the normal
> child.

Rules proposed to implement Section 504 made it clear that:

> The position of the Department with respect to this issue . . . is that neither cost nor other difficulty in complying are appropriate considerations in determining what practices constitute discrimination.

Argument 2: "The special education budget is limited."

A similar argument advanced by school personnel is that their expenditures for the handicapped are limited by their special education budget. Once that is committed for the year, they claim, no additional funds are available.

This argument is clearly rejected in *Mills,* but another helpful explanation can be found in the reasoning of a New Mexico Attorney General's Opinion issued December 22, 1971. It argues that children in special education are entitled to a free education just as much as other children, that handicapped children are entitled to free textbooks and transportation as long as any child is receiving them, and that therefore as long as any funds are available for the education of any child, funds must be available equally to the handicapped.

The argument by school personnel is really that they have chosen to put a certain amount of money into special education and to put other funds into other categories. If those special education funds run out, the school's priorities might have to be revised with a larger portion of the total budget invested in services to the handicapped.

Argument 3:   "The federal funds are limited."

An argument that is becoming popular is that the obligation to pay full costs has been created by federal laws but that the federal dollars are not sufficient to meet the need. Therefore, the argument goes, the school's obligation ends when the federal dollars run out. Or, to put it another way, since the federal funding is less than total, the school's effort at compliance can also be scaled down.

This issue was raised in hearings on Pub. L. 94-142 and soundly rejected by the United States Senate Committee on Labor and Public Welfare in S. Rep. No. 94-168 which accompanied that bill:

> The Committee rejects the argument that the Federal Govern-
> ment should only mandate services to handicapped children if, in
> fact, funds are appropriated in sufficient amounts to cover the
> full cost of the education. The Committee recognizes the State's
> primary responsibility to uphold the Constitution of the United
> States and their own state constitutions and state laws as well as
> the Congress' own responsibility under the Fourteenth Amend-
> ment to assure equal protection of the law.

Thus the duty to provide appropriate education to handicapped children is not conditioned on access to federal funds.

Argument 4:   "Schools should pay only a share."

Another argument is based on the common practice of allo-
cating specific amounts to cover any extra costs for a handicapped child. Therefore, if a child requires placement in a private
facility, the local school district would pay a certain amount and
ask for the state education agency to contribute a certain
amount. When the total contributed does not equal the total
cost to the parent, schools feel no obligation to make up the difference. The result is clearly discriminatory when the absence of
funds causes the child to be withdrawn from those needed, but
expensive, educational services.

A typical result is illustrated in the case of Daniel Kruse.
As explained in the complaint in *Kruse v. Campbell:*

> Daniel J. Kruse . . . is a learning disabled child . . . . For great
> numbers of handicapped children . . . the School Boards fail to
> operate appropriate programs of special education. Where no
> appropriate public program is available, the parents of the handi-
> capped children are eligible for a state tuition assistance grant to
> place the child in a private, special education program . . . . The
> great majority of "approved" private schools charge more for
> tuition than the maximum reimbursement grant allows. Upon
> information and belief, the tuition charged is usually as much as
> $2,000 to $3,000 in excess of the state tuition grant, and many
> times it is even more. Because of this scheme, the parents of
> "certified" handicapped children are forced to subsidize the tui-
> tion charged for private placements. All such parents are forced
> to pay a minimum of one quarter of the tuition and in most

cases, considerably more. For those parents who lack the financial resources to meet these costs, this usually means that the child cannot be enrolled in private school or that he or she is later dismissed from the private school when the parents default on their obligation to meet their share of the cost. Thus, the children of poor parents are totally denied the opportunity to obtain an appropriate education under this statutory scheme.

The Fairfax County Public Schools decided in November, 1974 and again in July, 1975 that Daniel's placement at the Herndon Intermediate School was inappropriate to his needs and that there was no other placement within the public school system which would be appropriate. Accordingly, the School Board approved a tuition grant in the amount of $1,250.00 for Daniel's placement in the Leary School . . . .

Daniel was thereafter accepted as a student by the Leary School. However, the tuition charged for Daniel's attendance is $4,645.00 per year.

This practice completely denies an opportunity for an appropriate education to those handicapped children of poor parents who cannot supplement tuition grants provided thereunder and for whom no appropriate, public educational program exists, while average children, handicapped children for whom appropriate, public educational programs exist, and handicapped children of affluent parents receiving state tuition grants receive an appropriate education at public expense. Such discrimination is invidious, arbitrary, capricious and without a rational and legitimate state purpose.

The federal court agreed and decision was rendered for plaintiff. On appeal, the Supreme Court vacated the judgment and remanded the case to the federal District Court with directions to decide the claim based on Section 504 (46 *U.S. Law Week* 3213, October 4, 1977). A similar result in Kruse's favor could be expected.

This practice is widespread and is the source of several pending lawsuits. As alleged in the complaint filed in *Crowder v. Riles,* the result is that:

> Parents of handicapped children must pay the amount that the act does not cover or must take their children out of school altogether or must accept placement of their children in inappropriate educational programs.

In *Beauchamp v. Jones* the complaint explains that Beauchamp was placed in a school charging $7,500 per year and was given a tuition grant of $1,380. When he could not pay the balance he was forced to withdraw from school and is still out of school. As the complaint summarizes it:

> [This practice] violates the equal protection clause of the Fourteenth Amendment of the United States Constitution, and as a result, also 42 U.S.C. 1983; in that the failure of the defendants to provide full reimbursement of the costs of the special education of all exceptional children required to attend private schools works an invidious discrimination against those unable to afford the additional cost of tuition at a private school. This discrimination results in the denial of an appropriate and adequate education, a benefit enjoyed by all normal children and some exceptional children for whom the State provides free education, and those exceptional children who attend private schools whose parents can afford to supplement the tuition reimbursement grant.

The merits of *Beauchamp* have not been decided but the complaint has been held to state a cause of action under 42 U.S.C. 1983 (*Beauchamp v. Jones*).

Clearly where the L.E.A. cannot meet a child's needs and places the child in another program, they must pay the full costs of that program. Section 504 states this obligation at 45 CFR 84.33(c)(1). Similarly, if the placement causes transportation costs, those costs must be paid so that any expense to the parent would be no greater than if the child were served in the program operated by the local school.

If the school cannot meet the child's needs and a residential placement is required, the school must pay for several things. Room and board and transportation costs must be provided at no expense to the parent. After all, if the local school could have done the job, there would be no room and board and transportation costs. Thus, those costs caused by the school's default cannot be assessed against the parent.

The public agency must also see that there is no cost to the parent for "the program including nonmedical care" according to Section 504 [45 CFR 84.33(c)(3)] and Pub. L. 94-142 [45 CFR 121a.302]. The "program" would include all specially designed instruction and related services such as counseling. Explanatory material accompanying the final Section 504 regulations, published at 42 Fed. Reg. 22691 (May 4, 1977), make it clear that psychological services and custodial and supervisory care must be provided at no expense to the parents. The only thing specifically excluded under both Acts is medical care. Medical services for diagnostic or evaluation purposes are to be provided at no expense to the parent, but medical care, such as corrective surgery, is not the responsibility of the school.

The law is not clear about psychiatric services. What if a learning disabled or emotionally disturbed child is placed in a residential facility and counseling services are carried out by a psychiatrist (a licensed M.D.) or under the general supervision of a psychiatrist? Does that make the counseling services medical care and therefore not the financial responsibility of the school? Although this has not been decided by any court yet, one could suggest a way to draw the line. If these counseling services are performed by someone who incidentally is an M.D., that does not make them "medical care." They would be "medical care," and no longer the financial responsibility of the school, only if the nature of the service was such that it could *only* be performed by an M.D.

This point is emphasized in an *amicus curiae* brief by James Todd and Peter Brooks of Advocacy, Incorporated, which was filed in the case of *Howard S. et al. v. Friendswood Independent School District et al.:* "The term 'medical' should be restricted to those services which may only be provided by or under the direction of a licensed physician or nurse so that the school would pay for the cost of any services such as psychotherapy, which are necessary to enable the student to benefit from education and which, though provided by a psychiatrist, could be provided by nonmedical personnel such as a psychologist or social worker. Federal courts have recognized that not all functions performed by psychiatrists are exclusively medical activities." (See also: *Jenkins v. United States; American Association of Marriage and Family Counselors v. Schlesinger.*)

In the case of the rest of the "program and nonmedical care," some schools are attempting to pay a percentage of costs on the grounds that their regular program extends from, for example, 8:30 to 3:30 P.M., 5 days a week, and they should pay only for the program offered in the residential facility during that time. Thus, some schools argue, costs of staff and activities in late afternoon, evening, and weekends would be charged to the parents. Nothing in the law supports this. Children are in the residential facility precisely because they could not be served by the school, 8:30 to 3:30 P.M., 5 days a week. They require more in the way of a "program" and the school must see this is furnished at no cost to the parents.

Argument 5: "The parents made the placement."

Another argument used by schools to justify not paying extra costs is that they are not responsible for the placement. The school argues that some children are in some other placement not because the school could not serve them but because the parents voluntarily placed them there. Under both Pub. L. 94-142 and Section 504, a voluntary placement would excuse the school from any financial obligation.

But the central question is what is a "voluntary" placement? If a child receives so little in the way of a program that the parents, in desperation, seek another placement, is that "voluntary"? No, the parent must have a choice between an "appropriate" educational offering at school and some other placement before the choice of the latter is considered voluntary. Who is to determine if that school offering was appropriate? Pub. L. 94-142 makes it a subject for an impartial due process hearing (see Chapter 8):

> Disagreements between a parent and a public agency regarding the availability of a program appropriate for the child, and the question of financial responsibility, are subject to the due process procedure. [45 CFR 121a.403(b)]

If at that hearing the school could show that what it had to offer was appropriate (not necessarily the best, or even as good as the other placement being considered by the parent), then the school would not bear any financial burden from the private placement.

However, when the school makes the recommendation of a residential placement, or tells the parent that the school cannot handle the child and that the parents must find some place for her, then the local school bears clear responsibility. A slightly different practice that in the past many schools have apparently engaged in is also going to make them financially responsible. Some schools have told this writer that when the parents asked for a residential placement because the child was too much for the parents to handle, the schools would agree. The schools felt they had not actually made a placement, but simply acquiesced in a decision already made by the parent. It came under the heading of doing the parent a favor. The placement was generally in a public agency and the local school was never faced with a financial consideration. Now, however, that decision would run counter to constitutional requirements of the least restrictive alternative (see Chapter 7), statutory requirements in the individual education plan (see Chapter 6), and also make the school financially responsible for any costs charged to the parents. Thus, whether the school recommends the placement or simply agrees to it, their ratification of the act makes them financially responsible.

Many questions will arise about this issue because of the number of parents who, prior to Pub. L. 94-142, sought out private residential placements for their children. Now those parents will predictably wish to keep their children in their current placement and start sending the bills to the school. The school's expected defense would be that they can now offer an appropriate education to the children. If that were true, the parent would have to send the child to the public school or continue to bear the financial burden of the private placement.

The issue again centers on appropriateness. The school would typically require a child to re-enroll in the school so that they could evaluate him and determine appropriate services. The parents would want their child to stay where he was currently doing well and not take the chance that, if the school had nothing appropriate, the child would then spend time on a waiting list to get back in the facility he had come from.

The parents should ask the public school to accept an

evaluation performed by the staff at the other facility. At an individual education program planning meeting the school can indicate what they would offer. The parent can then determine if the program is appropriate. If there is still disagreement, the matter should be taken to an impartial due process hearing as Pub. L. 94-142 contemplates. The hearing officer should be asked to order an independent evaluation of the child, with the participation of the school, the parents, and the staff of the other facility. On the basis of the evaluation, an individual education plan (see Chapter 6) would be drafted which would specify the services needed to meet the child's needs. The local school would then be examined to see if they have those services at an "appropriate" level. If they do, the hearing officer would be expected to find that costs of an alternative placement must be borne by the parent.

Even if the hearing officer finds that the school does not have an appropriate offering, the school still could put up a fight. They would argue that they have to pay the costs, but they would try to find a public program or a private program cheaper than the placement the parents are asking them to pay for. Hearing officers, and judges, if they are eventually required to hear the case, would probably side with the continuation of a successful placement rather than taking a chance on a new placement just to save the local school a few dollars. Schools that defaulted and did not aid the parents in their initial choice of a placement for the child will probably now be stuck with the parent's decision.

Argument 6: "Schools do not pay for therapy."

In order to avoid some costs schools have advanced the argument that they traditionally have not paid for some services like physical therapy. Pub. L. 94-142 requires not only special education but also related services that "are required to assist a handicapped child to benefit from special education" [45 CFR 121a.13(a)]. Pub. L. 94-142 lists 13 different categories of related services, which will be discussed in Chapter 5, and indicates they must be provided at no cost to the parent. Schools must become familiar with the list. They cannot refuse to provide some services just because they have never paid for that type of service before.

Some schools argue that whatever is offered in a placement that they have arranged for a child is all the parents are entitled to. One school district which provides speech therapy free in its own schools places cerebral palsied children in a private center which charges for speech therapy and which does not offer other needed services such as occupational therapy. Children do not have fewer rights in alternative placements. What they get in such placements must equal the full related services to which they are entitled. In the above case the public school would have to see that all related services were provided and that the parents were not charged.

A similar attempt at evasion occurs in school districts in which personnel are told in drafting the individual education plan to list only the two highest priority related services. There is no authority under federal law for a school to restrict related services in this way. All services required to assist the handicapped child to benefit from special education must be provided. Otherwise it is not a "free appropriate public education."

5 An "Appropriate" Public Education

It is a common feeling among educators that no one can accuse them of not offering an appropriate education because no one can define "appropriate." This belief would come as a surprise to judges who have been making decisions on right-to-education cases.

Terms used in defining "appropriate"

Pub. L. 94-142 defines an appropriate education in terms of specially designed instruction to meet the unique needs of a handicapped child, provided in conformity with an individual education program [20 U.S.C. 1401(16); 45 CFR 121a.4(d), 14(a)(1)]. Section 504 defines appropriate as the provision of regular or special education and related aids and services that are designed to meet individual educational needs of handicapped persons as adequately as the needs of nonhandicapped persons are met, and offered in an appropriate educational setting after proper evaluation and procedural safeguards [45 CFR 84.3(b)(1)].

There are thus several vital aspects of the definition of "appropriate": specially designed, conformity with an individual education plan, education as equally suitable as that offered the nonhandicapped, based on proper evaluation, attention to the educational setting, and procedural safeguards.

Landmark cases

These issues are well developed in a case that turns on the

question of appropriateness, *Fialkowski v. Shapp.* As summarized by Judge Huyett:

> Plaintiffs bring this action for damages claiming that defendant state and city officials have violated their rights to an appropriate education under the Equal Protection and the Due Process Clauses of the Fourteenth Amendment to the Constitution. Plaintiffs contend that, as multiple-handicapped children, they are denied equal protection under the Constitution because unlike the programs offered to normal and less severely retarded children, the nature of the educational programs offered them is such that no chance exists that the programs will benefit.

The Fialkowskis had the approximate intelligence of preschoolers, but they were placed in a program which emphasized skills such as reading and writing. This denied them instruction from which they could possibly benefit.

Defendants argued what many schools believe—that education is a privilege and not a right. Therefore, there is no right to education at all, let alone a right to an "appropriate" education. Defendants relied on the Supreme Court case of *San Antonio Independent School District v. Rodriguez.* That case involved an attack on a method of financing public education which resulted in such different expenditures between rich and poor school districts that students in the poor districts claimed they were being denied a constitutional right. The Supreme Court rejected the claim, holding that so long as schools offer minimally adequate educational opportunities to all, the fact that some students get much more does not violate the law. The *Rodriguez* case has been read by many to mean that there is no constitutional right to education.

But Judge Huyett distinguished *Rodriguez* on two important grounds. The first was that the Supreme Court assumed that the system would "provide each child with an opportunity to acquire the basic minimal skills necessary." But in *Fialkowski* the claim was that the instruction offered no chance for the plaintiffs to benefit and to acquire any basic skills. Judge Huyett thus held that although *Rodriguez* said that there was no constitutional right to a particular level of education (e.g., as good as that in the rich school district), there is "a constitutional right to a certain minimal level of education."

The second reason *Rodriguez* was not considered controlling in *Fialkowski* was that the *Rodriguez* court suggested that constitutional rights would be violated if the school operated "to the peculiar disadvantage of any suspect class." That court defined the characteristics of a suspect class as "saddled with such disabilities, or subjected to such a history of purposeful unequal treatment, or relegated to such a position of political powerlessness as to command extraordinary protection from the majoritarian political process." The *Fialkowski* court found the plaintiffs to be part of such a class. The Supreme Court of North Dakota similarly distinguished *Rodriguez* on the same basis in *Interest of G. H.*: "We are confident that the same Court would have held that GH's terrible handicaps were just the sort of 'immutable characteristics determined solely by the accident of birth' to which the 'inherently suspect' classification would be applied."

Thus, schools cannot content themselves with thinking that the Supreme Court has ruled that handicapped children do not have a right to a minimum level of education which offers the opportunity to acquire basic skills.

The next argument by the schools was that if they did, in fact, owe some minimum offering to the handicapped, it could be met by any offering whatsoever—it did not have to be special or "appropriate." That contention was adequately characterized by the attorneys in the Fialkowskis' petition for enforcement of the earlier decree as feeling that the "duty is merely to provide classroom space" and that any requirement for appropriateness is "surplusage not susceptible to interpretation" (Trial Brief filed August 1, 1977, page 3).

But without a suitable offering, one which offers the chance to benefit, there is no offering at all and even the "minimal" requirement has been violated. In *Lau v. Nichols*, Chinese-speaking students provided only with English language instruction sued the San Francisco schools. The Supreme Court found:

There is no equality of treatment merely by providing students with the same facilities, text books, teachers and curriculum; for students who do not understand English are effectively foreclosed from any meaningful education.

Basic English skills are at the very core of what these public schools teach. Imposition of a requirement that, before a child can effectively participate in the educational program, he must already have acquired those basic skills is to make a mockery of public education. We know that those who do not understand English are certain to find their classroom experiences wholly incomprehensible and in no way meaningful . . . .

Discrimination is barred which has that *effect* even though no purposeful design is present . . . . It seems obvious that the Chinese-speaking minority receives less benefits than the English-speaking majority from respondents' school system which denies them a meaningful opportunity to participate in the educational program.

The *Fialkowski* brief argues that without appropriate programs the handicapped, like the Chinese-speaking students, "are certain to find their classroom experiences wholly incomprehensible and in no way meaningful." The result is that the handicapped child is constructively excluded from educational opportunity. As characterized by plaintiffs' attorneys: "David and Walter Fialkowski were given access to buildings, rooms, and 'play-school' but they have been denied access to education."

Frederick L. v. Thomas dealt with a similar constructive exclusion. Children with specific learning disabilities alleged that they were discriminated against by the school's failure to provide instruction specially suited to their handicaps. In denying the school's motion to dismiss, Judge Newcomer summarized the problem:

Admittedly, most of the plaintiffs are afforded access to the same curriculum as normal children, but it is argued that the test of *equal* treatment is the suitability of the instructional services for the educational needs of the child. Many of the plaintiffs, it is said, cannot derive *any* educational benefit from the normal curriculum if that experience is not mediated by special instruction aimed at their learning handicaps. We are told that inappropriate educational placements predictably lead to severe frustration and to other emotional disturbances which impede the learning and erupt into antisocial behavior. On this basis it is argued that some or all of the class is constructively excluded from public educational services, because—for them—the instruction offered is virtually useless, if not positively harmful.

In finding for the plaintiffs, Judge Newcomer held that the defendants had violated the requirements of appropriateness and that they must follow certain standards in assessing needs and implementing programs. Those standards and procedures were already set out in the *P.A.R.C.* decree and, as summarized in the *Fialkowski* trial brief, they form the basis for the fullest definition of an appropriate educational offering:

> (a) the arrangement for complete detailed and precise multidisciplinary assessments for each mentally retarded child to form the basis for proper placement and an appropriate educational plan;
>
> (b) the provision of a written prescriptive educational program sufficient to guide, articulate and measure the delivery of individually appropriate education to each child in accordance with the diagnostic/prescriptive method;
>
> (c) timely and periodic reevaluation of individual education plans to insure that the program for each child is appropriate and responsive to his or her growth and learning potential;
>
> (d) systematic training for teachers and aides, in the diagnostic/prescriptive method, and other aspects of education for severely/profoundly retarded persons;
>
> (e) adequate supervision and assistance to teachers and classroom personnel and systematic superintendence of the organization of classes for the mentally retarded;
>
> (f) the formation of a plan establishing quality standards and the range and scope of programs for severely/profoundly retarded persons, and the organization of state and local education resources to effectuate that plan;
>
> (g) systematic monitoring of the delivery of appropriate education, enforcement of quality standards, and enforcement of the School Code.

All of the above taken together gives us a much fuller understanding of the essential terms used in defining "appropriate" in the statute: it must be specially designed instruction, it must follow proper evaluation, it must offer the student an opportunity to benefit, it must conform with the requirements of the individual education plan, there must be periodic reevaluation, the education must be as suitable as that offered to the nonhandicapped, it must be in the proper educational setting, and the school must observe procedural safeguards. Contrary to the defense claim in *Fialkowski,* appropriateness is not "surplusage not susceptible to interpretation."

Comparability problems: Limited program time

As schools seek to implement this requirement of appropriateness, one aspect of an appropriate education that may suffer is comparability. One reason for this is the limited amount of time per day offered in programing. Some handicapped children face the following type of day: a 2-hour bus ride in the morning, a short academic program, lunch, transportation to a facility for physical therapy, a short physical therapy program, transportation back to school, and a bus ride home. Some parents have computed their children's in-class time at less than an hour per day. Typically that allows attempted instruction in reading and mathematics, but no courses in history, geography, social studies, art, or physical education. And there is no opportunity for extracurricular activities. This certainly strains the notion of comparability.

The schools feel they are certainly making an appropriate offering which focuses on the child's immediate needs, and that there are just not enough hours in the day to offer transportation, therapy, and an academic program. One mother of a cerebral palsied child told me that she had been told that she had to choose between her child's intellectual or physical growth. That definitely violates comparability.

Some schools attempt to meet this problem in several ways: rerouting buses (long rides usually involve immense inefficiency); where the ride will still be long, placing an instructional aide on the bus; and where extra services such as physical therapy are needed, bringing the therapist to the children to lessen the time per day spent in transportation.

Less program time for the handicapped is often justified by schools on the grounds that it is as much time as the child can take. One program this writer visited sent autistic children home after one hour each day. Perhaps the children could take more, but the teachers could not.

What may be needed for "comparability" is an extra effort for the handicapped. The comparability notion does not work in reverse to bar additional resources. Explanatory information at 42 Fed. Reg. 32265 (June 24, 1977) accompanying regulations implementing Executive Order 11914 [Federal agency enforcement of Section 504, published at 41 Fed. Reg. 17871 (April 28, 1976) with implementing regulations at 45 CFR 85, at 42 Fed. Reg. 32264 (June 24, 1977)] states "in some situations, identical treatment of handicapped and nonhandicapped persons is not only insufficient but is itself discriminatory."

Comparability problems: Adequate personnel

Another stumbling block to comparability is the adequacy of instructional personnel. Services will clearly not be comparable or suitable if the teachers and their resources are not satisfactory. The Section 504 definition of "appropriate," stated in 45 CFR 84.33(b), is elaborated in explanatory material at 42 Fed. Reg. 22691 (May 4, 1977):

> Handicapped students' teachers must be trained in the instruction of persons with the handicap in question and appropriate materials and equipment must be available. The Department is aware that the supply of adequately trained teachers may, at least at the outset of the imposition of this requirement, be insufficient to meet the demand of all recipients. This factor will be considered in determining the appropriateness of the remedy for noncompliance with this section.

Thus, schools cannot merely place handicapped children in classrooms with state licensed personnel—the requirement is that the personnel must be specially trained in the handicap in question.

Schools were given 2 full years from the enactment of Pub. L. 94-142 to its first stage of implementation, and another year for full compliance. During those 3 years it was contemplated by Congress that schools would assess handicapped children to determine what needs existed in the district and then secure and/or train the required teachers. However, many schools have not done that. The regulations implementing Pub. L. 94-142 indicate at 45 CFR 121a.382-85 what is required for adequate personnel development.

First, there must be an annual needs assessment to determine if there are sufficient qualified persons for teaching and related services.

Second, it must be determined if needs can be met by retraining current personnel, or if new staff must be hired.

Third, the agency must determine the areas in which training needs to occur. The regulations clearly indicate this would include not only training in specific handicapping conditions but also training in writing individual education plans, nondiscriminatory testing, least restrictive alternatives, and procedural safeguards.

Fourth, the agency must indicate what school personnel need to receive the training. The regulations specifically include "speech teachers, regular teachers, administrators, psychologists, speech-language pathologists, audiologists, physical education teachers, therapeutic recreation specialists, physical therapists, occupational therapists, medical personnel, parents, volunteers, hearing officers, and surrogate parents."

Fifth, the agency must describe the content of the training. And the regulations require a search for "significant information and promising practices derived from educational research, demonstration, and other projects." Further, the state must have a system "designed to adopt, where appropriate, promising educational practices and materials proven effective through research and demonstration." Thus, the content of the training cannot be limited by local inadequacies. In one Texas program this writer visited, cerebral palsied children with motor impairment affecting their hands were not taught mathematics because the teacher said that she could not teach children who could not hold a pencil. The agency must search until they discover a way to train a teacher. They cannot say, as some currently do, that "no one here knows how to do it."

Sixth, the agency must indicate how the training will be

accomplished including the persons who will be used as training sources.

Seventh, there must be an indication of the schedule of training and from where the funds will come.

Finally, the personnel development plan must specify the procedures by which the training will be evaluated and how it will be determined whether program objectives were met.

The absence of such a personnel development plan is a clear signal that the school will not have personnel adequately trained to comply with the Act. Programs for the handicapped will then be neither suitable nor comparable. The final judgment whether a program is appropriate is a proper subject for an impartial due process hearing [45 CFR 121a.506(a), 504(a)(1)]. Time should not be spent in academic arguments on "appropriateness"–the problem should be taken up with an impartial hearing officer.

Access problems: Bureaucratic delay

Once the school does have a program which appears to meet the "free appropriate public education" criteria, problems can still arise if access to that program is interrupted in one of several ways.

The first interruption might be a bureaucratic delay. Scheduling a child for evaluation is not an evaluation. Completing the individual education plan and then scheduling the child for a placement does not meet the requirements of the law. Placing a child in a class and requesting aides or new equipment or scheduling the teacher for training does not satisfy the law. Under Section 504 and Pub. L. 94-142, after September 1, 1978, there can be no delay in providing full services. Programs delayed are programs denied.

Access problems: Summer vacation

A second type of interruption occurs with summer vacation. In regard to programs operated by the local education agency, and stopped during the summer, four arguments could be made. First, the equal protection argument described earlier indicates that a school might have to do more for some handicapped students in order to afford them equal opportunity. That seems clear in regard to amounts of money, staff ratios, and facilities. So why not unequal numbers of months of instruction? Why not 12 months per year for retarded or learning disabled children, for example, to give them an opportunity equal to that enjoyed in 9 months by nonhandicapped students? 45 CFR 84.4(b)(2) requires services to "afford handicapped persons equal opportunity to obtain the same result, to gain the same benefit, or to reach the same level of achievement."

Another equal protection argument would arise if the local school offered summer school to nonhandicapped children to help them catch up. Similarly, if the school offered year-round service to one disability category, they might now be required to offer it to all disability categories.

A third argument relates to the disjointed nature of services to the handicapped during the regular year. If required transportation and time for therapy mean that the average academic day of a handicapped student is only three-fourths of the nonhandicapped student's day, then why not extend the program year-round so 12 months for the handicapped might more nearly equal the services offered to others in 9 months.

A final argument relates to regression. A pending case in New York, *In the Matter of Richard G.*, was sent back for trial on the issue "whether his education would have regressed had he not participated in the summer program." If regression would occur, presumably the local school would have to offer a 12 month program or pay the costs of placement elsewhere. The issue of regression would certainly be a topic for an impartial hearing where the individual education plan proposed no summer services and the parent argued regression would occur.

One theory that might be advanced for determining the need for summer programs is attainment on the individual educational plan. For nonhandicapped children, a failing grade often leads to an offer of summer school remediation. For handicapped children, there might be a predetermined point on the individual education plan's annual goals below which the school would then offer summer services to increase attainment.

In regard to programs not operated by the local agency the

issue seems simpler. Where the agency has already made a determination that the child must be served elsewhere, and the program in which the child is placed is a 12 month offering, the local agency would have to pay as long as the child is there.

Access problems: Suspension and expulsion

Another way that access to a program is interrupted is through disciplinary suspensions or expulsions. This was a common practice attacked in *Mills:*

> Defendants shall not, on grounds of discipline, cause the exclusion, suspension, expulsion, postponement, interschool transfer, or any other denial of access to regular instruction in the public schools to any child for more than two days without first notifying the child's parent or guardian of such proposed action, the reasons therefore, and of the hearing before a Hearing Officer.

This issue—illegal exclusion under the guise of expulsion—has been dealt with in three recent federal cases. In *Davis v. Wynne* an educable retarded 17-year-old was expelled for disruptive behavior. The plaintiff complained that although he had been evaluated for special education and was entitled to special services, he was left in a regular program. He further claimed that the disruptive behavior was a symptom of his inappropriate placement and the frustration it caused. The plaintiff won his contention that not only must his expulsion be barred, but that he must return to a proper placement.

In *Donnie R. v. Wood* a 13-year-old boy was suspended for disciplinary reasons. Plaintiff argued that the offending behavior was due to his handicapped condition and that the school's action was discriminatory. The consent decree required the school to evaluate Donnie and place him in an appropriate program.

In *Stuart v. Nappi,* relying on Pub. L. 94-142, a court ruled a learning disabled child may not be expelled for disciplinary reasons, but must rather be considered for a change to a more appropriate placement. Plaintiff was a high school student with learning disabilities and a history of school behavioral problems. She had been evaluated as eligible for special education services and was placed in a program with one-to-one teaching. Her attendance became erratic and recommendations were made that a new placement committee meeting be held. A new program was prescribed in the spring of 1977 for the fall, but was not administered.

In mid-September 1977, plaintiff was involved in a school-wide disturbance and was suspended for 10 days. The Superintendent of Schools recommended that she be expelled for the remainder of the 1977-78 school year and she was scheduled to appear at a disciplinary hearing on November 30, 1977. On November 16 she made a request for a review of her special education program and on November 29 obtained a temporary restraining order to prevent the disciplinary hearing. The case that was finally decided was on the issue of an injunction to prevent the hearing.

The court ordered the injunction because, if the hearing were allowed, with an expulsion likely, irreparable harm would occur. First, there would be a delay in any kind of educational program while the special education committee met and planned a new one. The court noted that the special education department had not been very quick in the past and one could anticipate delay. Second, once a program was fashioned, it would, after expulsion, have to be carried out in a private school or in homebound instruction. The court noted its concern over the availability of a private placement and feared the plaintiff's education for the 1977-78 school year would be reduced to some type of homebound tutoring. "Such a result can only serve to hinder the plaintiff's social development and to perpetuate the vicious cycle in which she is caught."

Plaintiff also argued that she was being denied an appropriate public education. The court defined that term to mean "an educational program specially designed to meet her learning disabilities." The court found two reasons why that standard was not met. First, the program prescribed after the placement committee meeting was never carried out. Second, "the high school neglected to respond adequately when it learned the plaintiff was no longer participating in the special education program it had provided."

The denial of an appropriate education is important because it raises the question of whether the school's inappropriate treatment of the student caused the very behavior for which the school now sought to punish the child. The court concluded, "The Court cannot disregard the possibility that Danbury High School's handling of plaintiff may have contributed to her disruptive behavior."

Plaintiff raised another issue not previously decided by a federal court. Pub. L. 94-142 provides that:

> During the pendency of any proceedings conducted pursuant to this section, unless the state or local educational agency and the parents or guardian otherwise agree, the child shall remain in the then current educational placement of such child . . . until all such proceedings have been completed.

Plaintiff had filed a complaint and asked for review of her placement prior to the scheduled hearings. Thus, she had a right to remain in that placement until her complaint was resolved.

The court emphasizes that this places federal law in direct conflict with local policy regarding discipline. There appear to be only two exceptions to the law that handicapped children may not have a placement changed during the pendency of a special education complaint. The first is if the parents agree to it. In this case they clearly did not. The second case is if the children are "endangering themselves or others." The federal regulations would allow short-term emergency procedures to deal with such children, even during the pendency of a complaint. (The facts in *Stuart* showed no allegation of dangerousness.) But the court found the only acceptable short-term emergency procedure would be suspension—not expulsion. Thus, the court concluded, "the Handicapped Act establishes procedures which replace expulsion as a means of removing handicapped children from school if they become disruptive."

The court found further that even if plaintiff had not had a pending special education complaint, the school could not have legally expelled the child for two reasons. First, the expulsion would violate requirements that services be offered in the "least restrictive environment." To make this concept work, the schools must have a continuum of placements and choose one on the basis of appropriateness and the opportunity to interact with nonhandicapped children. The court found that expulsion would unduly limit the available range of placements since the likely placement for the plaintiff after expulsion would be at home. Changes in placement must be governed by the doctrine of the least restrictive environment. In the words of the *Stuart* court:

> The right to an education in the least restrictive environment may be circumvented if schools are permitted to expel handicapped children. An expulsion has the effect not only of changing a student's placement, but also of restricting the availability of alternative placements. For example, plaintiff's expulsion may well exclude her from a placement that is appropriate for her academic and social development. This result flies in the face of the explicit mandate of the Handicapped Act which requires that all placement decisions be made in conformity with a child's right to an education in the least restrictive environment.

The other reason expulsion of a handicapped child could not be legally accomplished is that it violates procedures established to change the placement of disruptive children. Pub. L. 94-142 recognizes that when a handicapped child's behavior is so disruptive that it interferes with the education of other children, a change in placement might be justified. But that change may be made only after certain procedures involving professional reevaluation of the situation and a decision that the new placement is appropriate to the child's needs. The court found that the expulsion procedures did not follow those steps, and therefore could not be used as a means of changing the placement of a disruptive handicapped child.

So where does that leave schools in their ability to deal with disruptive handicapped children? The *Stuart* court notes that its decision in no way affects the removal of students for all or part of a single class period for disciplinary reasons, but that more extensive discipline would be affected. In the court's words:

> It is important that the parameters of this decision are clear. The Court is cognizant of the need for school officials to be

vested with ample authority and discretion. It is, therefore, with great reluctance that the Court has intervened in the disciplinary process of Danbury High School. However, this intervention is of a limited nature. Handicapped children are neither immune from a school's disciplinary process nor are they entitled to participate in programs when their behavior impairs the education of other children in the program. First, school authorities can take swift disciplinary measures, such as suspension, against disruptive handicapped children. Second, a . . . [professional team] can request a change in the placement of handicapped children who have demonstrated that their present placement is inappropriate by disrupting the education of other children. The Handicapped Act thereby affords schools with both short-term and long-term methods of dealing with handicapped children who are behavioral problems.

A new tendency exists in schools to use "Alternative Study Centers," or some other euphemistically named place, to send students for "in-school suspensions." These are used, admittedly, to avoid the procedures required for out of school suspensions and expulsions. But schools must be aware that they cannot casually or frequently interrupt access to services of a handicapped child without violating federal law. As *Mills* summed it up—the law's concern is not just over acts officially denoted as "expulsion" but over any "exclusion, suspension, expulsion, postponement, interschool transfer, or any other denial of access."

Access problems: Full range of services

Access must not only be continuing, but there must also be access to the full range of services required to make a program effective. An ineffective program is a denial of a free appropriate public education and related services. Related services are those required services that assist a child in benefiting from the program. Pub. L. 94-142's regulations list 13 related services:

(1) "Audiology" includes:
(i) Identification of children with hearing loss;
(ii) Determination of the range, nature, and degree of hearing

loss, including referral for medical or other professional attention for the habilitation of hearing;

(iii) Provision of habilitative activities, such as language habilitation, auditory training, speech reading (lip-reading), hearing evaluation, and speech conservation;

(iv) Creation and administration of programs for prevention of hearing loss;

(v) Counseling and guidance of pupils, parents and teachers regarding hearing loss; and

(vi) Determination of the child's need for group and individual amplification, selecting and fitting an appropriate aid, and evaluating the effectiveness of amplification.

(2) "Counseling services" means services provided by qualified social workers, psychologists, guidance counselors, or other qualified personnel.

(3) "Early identification" means the implementation of a formal plan for identifying a disability as early as possible in a child's life.

(4) "Medical services" means services provided by a licensed physician to determine a child's medically related handicapping condition which results in the child's need for special education and related services.

(5) "Occupational therapy" includes:

(i) Improving, developing or restoring functions impaired or lost through illness, injury, or deprivation;

(ii) Improving ability to perform tasks for independent functioning when functions are impaired or lost; and

(iii) Preventing, through early intervention, initial or further impairment or loss of function.

(6) "Parent counseling and training" means assisting parents in understanding the special needs of their child and providing parents with information about child development.

(7) "Physical therapy" means services provided by a qualified physical therapist.

(8) "Psychological services" include:

(i) Administering psychological and educational tests, and other assessment procedures;

(ii) Interpreting assessment results;

(iii) Obtaining, integrating, and interpreting information about child behavior and conditions relating to learning;

(iv) Consulting with other staff members in planning school

programs to meet the special needs of children as indicated by psychological services, including psychological counseling for children and parents.

(9) "Recreation" includes:

(i) Assessment of leisure function;

(ii) Therapeutic recreation services;

(iii) Recreation programs in schools and community agencies; and

(iv) Leisure education.

(10) "School health services" means services provided by a qualified school nurse or other qualified person.

(11) "Social work services in schools" includes:

(i) Preparing a social or developmental history on a handicapped child;

(ii) Group and individual counseling with the child and family;

(iii) Working with those problems in a child's living situation (home, school, and community) that affect the child's adjustment in school; and

(iv) Mobilizing school and community resources to enable the child to receive maximum benefit from his or her educational program.

(12) "Speech pathology" includes:

(i) Identification of children with speech or language disorders;

(ii) Diagnosis and appraisal of specific speech or language disorders;

(iii) Referral for medical or other professional attention necessary for the habilitation of speech or language disorders;

(iv) Provisions of speech and language services for the habilitation or prevention of communicative disorders; and

(v) Counseling and guidance of parents, children, and teachers regarding speech and language disorders.

(13) "Transportation" includes:

(i) Travel to and from school and between schools,

(ii) Travel in and around school buildings, and

(iii) Specialized equipment (such as special or adapted buses, lifts, and ramps), if required to provide special transportation for a handicapped child.

As stated in the regulations at the end of the definition:

The list of related services is not exhaustive and may include other developmental, corrective or supportive services (such as

artistic and cultural programs, and art, music, and dance therapy),
if they are required to assist a handicapped child to benefit from
special education.

No one child may need all these services, but where a
service is needed and not made available there will likely be a
denial of access to an appropriate program. Schools cannot simply say that they do not provide that kind of service. And they
cannot limit a child to, for example, the two most needed related services. Similarly, where the service offered is wholly
inadequate (e.g., physical therapy 30 minutes twice a week for a
cerebral palsied child when one hour per day is prescribed by
the physician) there may still be a denial of an appropriate
education.

Access problems: Physical education

Physical education is defined in Pub. L. 94-142 regulations
as meaning:

> . . . the development of: (A) Physical and motor fitness; (B)
> Fundamental motor skills and patterns; and (C) Skills in aquatics,
> dance and individual and group games and sports (including intra-
> mural and lifetime sports). The term includes special physical
> education, adapted physical education, movement education, and
> motor development.

This breadth is important for two reasons. First, many
handicapped children are simply excluded from physical education. Physical therapy is considered their physical education. It
is not. Physical education is part of the educational program
and all handicapped children must be included, with physical
education as part of each individual education plan.

Second, some orthopedically impaired children who do
not need specially designed instruction in the academic program
are excluded from physical education on the grounds they
could not benefit; yet they are not provided physical therapy
because they are not considered to be in special education.
Their parents often have fought for years to keep them out of
special education because the price of that classification is
usually segregation from their academic peers and placement in

a program with handicapped children completely unsuited to them. Under Pub. L. 94-142 and Section 504 those children should be considered in special education solely for the purposes of an adapted physical education program and in regular classes for the rest of the day. If the physical education staff has not traditionally been providing motor skill training to the handicapped, they must be trained how to do so. The breadth of the definition of physical education means that it includes virtually all children.

Access problems: Extracurricular activities

Another area in which schools often bypass the handicapped is in extracurricular activities. The school's obligation here does not proceed from the notion of a free appropriate education, for extracurricular activities are not related to specially designed instruction. But Section 504 makes clear that federally assisted programs

> . . . shall provide nonacademic and extracurricular services and activities in such manner as is necessary to afford handicapped students an equal opportunity for participation in such services and activities. Nonacademic and extracurricular services and activities may include counseling services, physical recreational athletics, transportation, health services, recreational activities, special interest groups or clubs sponsored by the recipient . . . . [a] recipient that offers physical education courses or that operates or sponsors interscholastic, club, or intramural athletics shall provide to qualified handicapped students an equal opportunity for participation in these activities. [45 CFR 84.37(a) (1), (2); (c)(1)]
>
> The most immediate requirements will be to have services and activities in places accessible to the handicapped and to provide transportation that is needed. For example, schools that bus the handicapped home in the afternoon must make some of those buses available for the handicapped who wish to stay and participate in an extracurricular or nonacademic service. Where such an activity involves a weekend trip and the school is furnishing transportation to the nonhandicapped, it must also arrange transportation for the handicapped.

6 Individualized Education Program

A unique contribution of Pub. L. 94-142 is the requirement of an individual education plan for every child receiving special education services. A plan must be in effect at the beginning of each school year for any child who will receive special education during that school year. For handicapped children identified during the year, an individual education planning meeting must be held within 30 calendar days of the determination that special services are needed. The plan is then to be implemented immediately.

Local school's participation

The local education agency must participate in writing the plan in the following situations: first, when the child will be served in a local education agency program; second, when the local education agency places the child in a program operated elsewhere. An alternative placement cannot be made until a plan has been drawn up. Only then will the agency know where the child needs to be served. 45 CFR 121a.552(c) indicates that the child must be served in the local school unless the plan "requires some other arrangement." It is not unusual for private schools to be sent a child with a poor evaluation and no individual education plan. This is an illegal placement and the private school should not become an accomplice. A private facility should require the school to complete the evaluation and the individual plan. (Any evaluation the private school eventually has to perform in order to produce an appropriate program should be billed to the school, not to the parents.) When the plan is annually revised, local school and private program people work in conjunction. But in the beginning, until a plan is drawn up, the local school cannot be sure that another facility will even be involved.

Third, when a child is already being served elsewhere and the local agency agrees to that arrangement, the local school is responsible for seeing that a plan is written and for annually participating in its review. Fourth, when a child is in some private facility that does not meet the child's special education needs, the local school must make available "genuine opportunities to participate in special education and related services" [45 CFR 121a.452(b)] and if the child does in fact receive services from the local school then the local school must "initiate and conduct meetings to develop, review, and revise an individualized education program for the child" [45 CFR 121a.348(a)]. Some children will be in private or parochial schools and will not choose to have any contact with the local school. In that case, no individual plan would be required.

Parent's participation

Much of the Congressional discussion during passage of Pub. L. 94-142 focused on the need to include parents in making decisions about their child. Thus, a joint planning conference is required annually. Out of that conference comes the written statement of the individual plan for the next year. Some schools are already developing the pattern of scheduling 15 minute annual planning meetings with parents. This is not the "joint conference" that Pub. L. 94-142 had in mind. Worse, some schools begin the meeting by handing the parents a photocopied copy of the plan, strongly suggesting that no input from them is needed or desired.

Meetings really should be joint conferences with all participants having a general outline of what should be proposed, but each willing to learn from the other. The participants at the meeting are specified in Pub. L. 94-142 in five categories. Procedures for participation are at 45 CFR 121a.344-45.

First, the school must be represented by at least two persons, although at their discretion they can include more. One has to be qualified to provide or supervise special education. The other has to be the child's teacher. "Teacher" is defined as the regular teacher of the child who has never had any special education services, or the special education teacher or resources person if the child is receiving services. If the child has never been in school, the school shall simply designate a teacher to participate, but presumably it would be a teacher expected to provide services after the plan is written. Thus, one school representative is supposed to have instructional contact with the child. The school personnel must meet these requirements and should be able to answer the parents' questions. Presumably the parents could challenge the appropriateness of any of the school personnel and take the issue to an impartial hearing. The parents may object, for example, to a school's claim that the principal is their special education representative. The parents may not feel a school's principal is an appropriate representative.

Second, either or both of the child's parents may be there.

Third, the child may be there "where appropriate." No standard is suggested to indicate how to make the determination of appropriateness or who must make it. *Hairston v. Drosick* ordered that the child should make the determination of appropriateness at hearings and perhaps the same logic would apply to a planning meeting. Certainly the trends in *Goss v. Lopez, Tinker v. Des Moines,* and *In Re Gault* would suggest that older children should be there. In the absence of any definite policy it can be expected that schools will probably leave it up to the parents.

Fourth, other individuals may be involved at the discretion of the parents or the school.

Fifth, if a child has been evaluated for the first time prior to this planning meeting, there must also be a member of the evaluation team or some other school representative knowledgeable about the specific evaluation procedures used with the child and familiar with the evaluation itself.

It is possible to have a planning meeting without the parents' participation. The plans are not contracts and no one has to sign them. So if parents do not object and do not ask for a hearing, a plan could be written without them, mailed to them (complying with notice requirements for a placement), and no response from them would be required.

The one exception is if the plan is for the child's first placement. If so, the parents would have to consent to the plan's recommendation [45 CFR 121a.504(b)(ii)], although they still would not have to participate in the planning meeting.

The school must attempt, however, to get the parents there and must document those attempts. They must notify parents well in advance of the purpose, time, place, and who will be in attendance. Parents may ask for a rescheduling and the school must attempt to arrange a mutually agreed on time and place. The notice may be oral or written or both, but a record must be kept of it. If the parents still cannot attend, the school may attempt to get their participation through telephone contact.

If the school goes ahead without parents in attendance, they must document the efforts to arrange parental participation including: (a) detailed records of phone calls, (b) copies of correspondence sent and received, and (c) records of visits made to the parents' home or place of business and any results.

If parents do attend they must be notified that they have a right to bring other persons at their discretion. The school must take steps to insure that any barrier to parental understanding is removed, for example, interpreters should be provided for those parents who speak English as a second language, or who use sign language. After the meeting the parents must be given a complete copy of the plan if they request it.

Assessment and annual goals

The contents of the plan are specified at 45 CFR 121a.346. The plan must begin with a statement of the child's present level of educational performance. The full range of disabilities for which the child must be assessed [45 CFR 121a.532(f)] and the range of related services for which assessment must have been made [45 CFR 121a.13(b)(1)-(11)] indicate that the term "educational performance" is very broad and must provide a baseline which reflects the entirety of the assessment. The proposed regulations [published at 41 Fed.

Reg. 56986 (Dec. 30, 1976)] specified that the statement must reflect academic achievement, social adaptation, prevocational and vocational skills, psychomotor skills, and self-help skills. The sense of the final regulations would still require all that.

The plan must include a statement of annual goals including short-term instructional objectives to take the child from the present level of educational performance to the annual goal. Some schools have started the practice of developing an "overall plan" in the joint conference in the spring and then letting the teachers fill in the short-term objectives after the program gets started in the fall. This means that the teacher would be starting not only without the legally required plan in effect at the beginning of the school year [45 CFR 121a.342(a)], but also that the teacher would be wasting the child's time. The Senate Committee on Labor and Public Welfare recognized in S. Rep. No. 94-168 that "in many instances the process of providing special education and related services to handicapped children is not guaranteed to produce any particular outcome." A teacher operating without instructional objectives would not be heading toward any predictable outcome. Pub. L. 94-142 requires the goal statement and interim objectives not as a guarantee and not as a contract, but as "a written record of reasonable expectations" which may be monitored and cause the program to be constantly revised in order to produce the expected outcome.

Specific services provided

The individual education plan must also state "the specific special education and related services to be provided to the child." This is easily the most hotly contested section in all of the regulations. The proposed regulations required "a statement of specific educational services needed by the child (determined without regard to availability)." Many educators realized what a statement "of need without regard to availability of services" would look like in comparison to the services they were planning to give handicapped children, and they were afraid some contractual obligation might be implied upon which they could be sued.

After intense pressure, the Office of Education simply reiterated the specific statutory language—"services to be provided"—and noted in a comment published at 42 Fed. Reg. 42508 (Aug. 23, 1977):

> The Office of Education has decided that some experience operating under the statute would be useful before considering whether further regulations on this point would be appropriate.

That "experience operating under the statute" quickly revealed that schools were cutting back on the educational plans and making what was to be provided the same as what they had available. In one example called to the Office of Education's attention, a school which did not intend to make physical therapy services available to cerebral palsied children simply did not evaluate for physical therapy needs, did not state anything about motor skills in the level of educational performance, and then logically omitted physical therapy from the list of services to be provided.

Realizing this situation needed to be corrected, Edwin Martin, Chief of the Bureau of Education for the Handicapped, wrote all chief state school officers to explain that the interpretation that the final regulations mean that a public agency must provide to a handicapped child only those services that are available in the agency is not correct. Section 504 and Pub. L. 94-142 and their implementing regulations require that by September 1, 1978, each handicapped child must be provided all services necessary to meet his or her special education and related needs. Thus, the individual plan must state all services needed by the child.

Participation in regular programs

The plan must also indicate the extent to which the child will be able to participate in regular educational programs. Every conceivable part of the day should be examined including class work, meals, recess periods, physical education, counseling services, and recreational activities to determine those things in which the handicapped student may participate with the non-handicapped. The child must participate in all activities with the nonhandicapped "unless a handicapped child's individualized education program requires some other arrangement" [45 CFR 121a.552(c)]. The joint planning conference should consider all activities and make a decision. They should not leave it up to the school to decide later what activities the child should be involved in.

The plan must state the projected date for initiating services and the anticipated duration of each service. This will provide a safeguard against waiting lists and other delays in the beginning of services. It can also be a planning aid because if a school expects one type of service to be needed for a specific duration, then they should be expected to be ready to begin the second level of service activity upon the successful conclusion of the first.

Annual criteria and evaluation procedures

Finally, the plan must state "appropriate objective criteria and evaluation procedures and schedules for determining, on at least an annual basis, whether the short term instructional objectives are being achieved" [45 CFR 121a.346(e)]. Since the plan was developed in a joint conference with parents and is annually reviewed by a group including parents, the criteria and evaluation procedures must be understandable to parents. Parents who do not understand them, or disagree with their appropriateness, should certainly attempt to have them changed either in the planning meeting or afterward at an impartial due process hearing.

Accountability

The individualized education plan must govern the provision of services to the child and the decision where those services are to be offered. Schools are accountable for offering the services called for by the plan, although they are not accountable if a child does not achieve the annual goal so long as the appropriate services have been offered. This rather misunderstood distinction is clarified in 45 CFR 121a.349 and its following comments.

Each public agency must provide special education and related services to a handicapped child in accordance with an individualized education program. However, Part B of the Act does not require that any agency, teacher or other person be held accountable if a child does not achieve the growth projected in the annual goals and objectives.

Comment. This section is intended to relieve concerns that the individualized education program constitutes a guarantee by the public agency and the teacher that a child will progress at a specified rate. However, this section does not relieve agencies and teachers from making good faith efforts to assist the child in achieving the objectives and goals listed in the individualized education program. Further, the section does not limit a parent's right to complain and ask for revisions of the child's program, or to invoke due process procedures, if the parent feels that these efforts are not being made.

7 The Least Restrictive Alternative

Services to the handicapped child must always be offered in a setting which deviates least from the regular nonhandicapped program. This is because any alternative chosen must be seen as "restrictive." It restricts the way teachers, family, and peers view the child. It may restrict the opportunity for the child to interact freely with others. And, of course, a mistaken placement or a poor program could injure the child's chances to be self-supporting and integrated into society.

"Restrictive"

In applying the concept of "least restrictive," little attention is given to defining the term "restrictive." The federal regulations recognize one element at 45 CFR 121a.552(d) when they require consideration of "any potential harmful effect." One good example would be the stigma of being treated differently. In one Texas school, handicapped children currently being served in their neighborhood school were proposed to be bussed to a nearby school for services that on paper appeared to be better. But it would cause these children to stand outside and wait for a bus as their peers go into school, then arrive late at the new school and go into the only self-contained area in an otherwise "open" school. The stigma was immediately apparent to the children. Such a "potential harmful effect" might make that alternative too restrictive and therefore unsuitable.

Another type of restriction is medication. Some schools consider placing a medicated child in a regular classroom as being the least restrictive alternative. But chemical restraints are highly restrictive. They do not educate, remediate, or habilitate. For some children they eliminate a problem that has an adverse effect on educational performance, but for the vast majority the effect is to interfere with education and also to cause long-term harmful side effects. The reality is that the child is being chemically restrained to meet the needs of staff not trained to deal with certain behaviors, and that is too restrictive.

The right to be free of restrictions

A child has a right to be free of alternative education restrictions under the Constitution unless due process of law is followed. And courts have held that due process requires that in employing restrictions the least drastic means must be used. In *Shelton v. Tucker* the Supreme Court stated:

> Even though the governmental purpose be legitimate and substantial, that purpose cannot be pursued by means that broadly stifle fundamental personal liberties when the end can be more narrowly achieved. The breadth of legislative abridgement must be viewed in the light of less drastic means for achieving the same basic purpose.

Thus, even if the proposed alternative is the proper place for the child and the best place to offer services, the child must still be guaranteed that it is the least restrictive alternative. This definitely contradicts traditional practices in special education. For many years it has been the practice, when a student was identified as in need of special help, to place the child in a separate facility. Wherever the program was located, it was probably composed of similarly handicapped students.

Segregation harmful: Integration beneficial

Special educators and others have learned that segregation is not the best way to deal with every handicapped child. There might be short-term benefits to segregation of the handicapped (and it might certainly be easier for the administrators), but the long-term problems are now apparent. The recent case of *Hairston v. Drosick* summarized the problem.

A child's chance in this society is through the educational process. A major goal of the educational process is the socialization
process that takes place in the regular classroom, with the result-
ing capability to interact in a social way with one's peers. It is
therefore imperative that every child receive an education with
his or her peers insofar as it is at all possible . . . . [P]lacement of
children in abnormal environments outside of peer situations imposes additional psychological and emotional handicaps upon
children which, added to their existing handicaps, causes them
greater difficulties in future life.

Congress recognized this and Senator Stafford, the author
of an important amendment to prevent segregation of the
handicapped, stated: "We are concerned that children with
handicapping conditions be educated in the most normal possible and least restrictive setting, for how else will they adapt to
the world beyond the educational environment, and how else
will the nonhandicapped adapt to them?" [120 Cong. Rec. S
8438 (May 20, 1974)].

The case of *Mattie T. v. Holladay* offered expert testimony
as to the harm done by segregation. The plaintiff's brief for
summary judgment included a portion of the affidavit of Dr.
Milton Budoff, an authority on the education of the handicapped:

In the course of my work over the past 24 years I have become
increasingly concerned about the harmful and inhumane effects
of separating and isolating children who are mentally retarded or
otherwise handicapped from the rest of society. The separation is
usually justified as necessary to the provision of better special
education or treatment programs. However, the education and
treatment programs that have been provided in a great many of
these separate institutions, schools and "special" classes have
been woefully inadequate and, at times, scandalously inhumane.
The major reason institutions for the mentally retarded and so-
called special schools for the handicapped have been located away
from the population centers is so that "normal" people will not
be "oppressed" by the needs of these persons. And for similar
reasons, school districts have created "special" so-called "self-
contained" classes for mentally retarded and handicapped chil-

dren (when they have allowed such children to attend school at all) and located them in separate buildings, trailers or in basements.

There is nothing about quality education or treatment for the vast majority of these children that necessitates their removal from the normal activities of the mainstream of society. Furthermore, the harm that flows from not learning to live within a community, not working and playing with nonhandicapped children the same age, is so great that placement in an isolated special school or class (and certainly an institution) cannot be justified, except in the most severe cases for whom particular intensive specialized services are necessary. My work on the two Massachusetts councils has shown me that with a proper state effort appropriate educational services in normal settings for handicapped children can be provided, and in fact must be provided if these children are to become independent, contributing members of society.

Dr. Budoff goes on to describe the benefits of an integrated program for handicapped and nonhandicapped children.

[M]entally retarded children gain a better understanding of proper social behavior by being in close contact with nonhandicapped children their own age who function normally within society, than by copying the aberrant behavior patterns that the mentally retarded children, usually of a variety of ages, evidence in the segregated special class. In addition there are several other consequences of being in an integrated program that can lead to academic benefits for the mentally retarded child: the development of a more positive self-image by not having to attend a program perceived as separate from and inferior to that of his siblings and neighbors; exposure to and awareness of, even peripherally, a more advanced and diverse curriculum; and constant contact with stimulating and challenging academic role models in more advanced peers. All children, and especially mentally retarded children, learn a great deal socially and academically from their peers and the importance of contact with appropriate role models cannot be stressed too much.

In my experience, nonhandicapped children have not been harmed by the presence of handicapped children in their classrooms. In fact, they too can benefit from this contact by learning how to get along with and appreciate a wider variety of children than they are now accustomed to. This development of a tolerance for differences in people is important to the process of growing up.

Variety of alternatives and individual determination

The brief in *Mattie T. v. Holladay* then sums up the federal response intended to prevent segregation:

> The Bureau of Education for the Handicapped Guidelines establish, *inter alia,* two important steps to be taken by school districts . . . . 1) "a variety of program alternatives (e.g., continuum of education services) must be available in every L.E.A. [local education agency] to meet the varying needs of handicapped children" and 2) an individual determination of the appropriate program alternatives must be made for each child in conformance with the procedures for nondiscriminatory evaluations.

This two step procedure—having a full range of alternatives and considering each case individually—is not followed in many school districts. The recent case of *Hairston v. Drosick* illustrates this problem.

> The plaintiff child, Trina Evet Hairston, has a condition known as spina bifida which has left said plaintiff with a minor physical impairment which includes incontinence of the bowels and a noticeable limp. The child is clearly physically able to attend school in a regular public classroom. The plaintiff child is of normal mental competence and capable of performing easily in a regular classroom situation.
>
> At the time the plaintiff child was to begin this school year, the plaintiff child was not wanted in the regular classroom and it was made clear to the plaintiff Sheila Hairston that the child was not to be permitted to attend Gary Grade School without her mother's intermittent presence.
>
> The requirement of the plaintiff's mother's intermittent presence at Gary Grade School as a condition of her child's being permitted to attend Gary Grade School, coupled with the impossibility of this request upon the plaintiff Sheila Hairston, constituted an exclusion of the plaintiff child from Gary Grade School . . . . even if the mother's presence were circumstantially possible, the right of a child to attend school cannot be legally conditioned

upon the mother's presence at the school. The needless exclusion of these children and other children who are able to function adequately from the regular classroom situation would be a great disservice to these children . . . . A child has to learn to interact in a social way with its peers and the denial of this opportunity during his minor years imposes added lifetime burdens upon a handicapped individual.

The educational fact that handicapped children should be excluded from the regular classroom situation only as a last resort is recognized in federal law. The federal statute providing moneys to states for special education programs mandates that every state have procedures to assure handicapped children are educated with children who are not handicapped and that removal of handicapped children from the regular education environment occurs only when the nature or severity of the handicap is such that education in regular classes with the use of supplementary aids and services cannot be achieved satisfactorily.

The Court, after careful review of the facts and applicable law, concluded that:

> The exclusion of a minimally handicapped child from a regular public classroom situation without a bona fide educational reason is in violation of Title V of Public Law 93-112, "The Rehabilitation Act of 1973," 29 U.S.C. 794.

The range of alternatives

To avoid placing the handicapped child in a setting that is too restrictive, and to meet the federal guidelines, the school must offer at least a minimum range of alternatives. The range includes:

(1) The regular classroom. Placement in the regular classroom must be legitimately considered for each child.

(2) The regular classroom with itinerant instruction. "Supplemental aids and services" in the regular classroom should be attempted before a more restrictive setting can be justified.

(3) The regular classroom for all academic and nonacademic programs possible and the resource room for the remainder of the activities.

(4) Full time in a special class in a neighborhood school which has nonhandicapped children.

(5) Assignment to a special school as close to the child's home as possible.

(6) Educational services provided in a nonschool setting such as home, hospital, or institution. (45 CFR 121a.551)

Under Pub. L. 94-142, if there is not a full continuum of services available, the school must attempt a consolidation with neighboring districts. If the needed services are still not available, they are to be provided directly by the state. Schools must clearly move away from the old habit of placing a child in whatever services are already available; they must create the full range of services needed.

Lack of funds no excuse for restrictions

Many federal courts have been asked to rule about children in settings which are unduly restrictive. Invariably the defendant's argument is that it costs too much money to set up a full range of alternatives. Federal courts consistently ignore that plea as any justification to deny individual rights to service in the least restrictive setting, and usually order the creation of other alternatives. One recent decision, *J. L. v. Parham*, even pointed out that the creation of less restrictive alternatives was not only constitutionally mandated, but that it would also save the state money.

Administrative inconvenience no excuse for restrictions

Assuming that the proper alternatives are available, the decision of which one in which to place a child must be an individual decision. A school cannot have a policy that all educable mentally retarded children would go into a special educable mentally retarded class, or that all cerebral palsied children would automatically be contracted out to a cerebral palsy facility, or that all learning disabled children would automatically be mainstreamed. They must take each case on its merits.

This means schools must rethink every placement currently made and relate it specifically to the requirements of the individual education plan. The case of *Hairston v. Drosick* is highly illustrative. That case involved a little girl who was ready to start school but had a noticeable limp and incontinence of the bowels due to the condition known as spina bifida. The administration refused to admit her to a regular classroom and insisted that she had to go into a program for the handicapped.

The federal court rejected that argument. Why did the educational needs of the child dictate placement anywhere but the regular classroom? Clearly the school's decision reflected only administrative convenience. The court stated that exclusion from the regular classroom was a last resort, to be used only "when the nature or severity of the handicap is such that education in regular classes with the use of supplementary aids and services cannot be achieved satisfactorily." To place the child elsewhere, the court found, there must be a compelling educational justification. Administrative convenience does not meet this test. Parents and schools must make sure that the individual education plan satisfactorily indicates the justification for the placement.

Architectural barriers no excuse for restrictions

One factor which often wrongly influences the placement decision is the presence of architectural barriers. Curbs, narrow doors, lack of elevators, inaccessible restrooms, and fear about evacuation in case of emergencies lead some administrators to automatically bar children in wheelchairs or wearing leg braces. They are often sent to a new barrier-free facility which, in one sense of the word, is less restrictive. But, in the more important constitutional sense, such segregation may be unduly restrictive.

Federal law now requires that programs be made accessible to the handicapped. Alterations may be possible, such as building ramps, handrails, and automatic doors. Classes can be reassigned to the first floor. The entire facility does not need to be made accessible and every bathroom and every door altered. But enough must be done so that a child will not be automatically barred on the basis of physical obstacles.

Where more substantial structural changes are needed for program accessibility, the agency has until June, 1980, to complete the job. But by December, 1977, they must, in consultation with handicapped persons, have drawn up a transition plan which is available to the public and which identified the obstacles, described the methods to be used to make the program accessible, and specified the schedule. Of course, all facilities constructed from June, 1977, on must be barrier free.

I recently visited a school system that has been barrier free for over 20 years. A school system which really cares about these things can do it.

Inadequate staff no excuse for restrictions

A final barrier to implementation of this doctrine is that a school has an inadequate staff. Consider three typical examples. First, a child is being educated with the nonhandicapped in elementary school, but upon graduation to a secondary school is segregated because no teacher is trained to deal with him adequately. Second, a child is properly placed in a segregated program so that his educational functioning can be raised enough to be reintegrated. However, the staff is inadequate and improvement does not occur, so the child must stay segregated. Third, a child is properly placed in a regular classroom, but the teacher is ill-prepared, cannot handle the child, the education of nonhandicapped children is affected, and the handicapped child eventually loses interest and is expelled for erratic attendance.

Pub. L. 94-142 recognizes that staff training is vital to this process and mandated the comprehensive personnel development plan detailed in Chapter 4. Administrators must have systems to discover staff weaknesses, and once they are discovered, the weaknesses must be remediated.

Emergency placements

There are still some areas which are in great flux at the time of this writing. One of these areas has to do with the decision when to place a child who, upon first contact, appears to need something other than a regular classroom. Pub. L. 94-142 requires that the individual be served in the regular classroom unless supplementary aids and services have been attempted and were unsatisfactory. For a child to be placed in special education requires first an evaluation and then an individual education program plan which will determine where the placement should be. All that takes time. What if a professional truly feels it would not serve the child, or the children in the regular classroom, to begin services there?

Schools seem to be following three alternatives. First, some schools tell the parents to keep the child home until he can be evaluated and an individual education planning conference can be convened. This is clearly a denial of services and the fact that many parents, uninformed of their rights, will agree to it, does not excuse the illegality.

Second, schools might recommend a temporary placement which they honestly think is best and ask for parental agreement. The comprehensive evaluation must occur as quickly as possible so that an individual plan may be drawn up within 30 calendar days of the beginning of the temporary placement. That plan would then govern services and placement for the remainder of the year.

Third, some schools are treating the initial "diagnostic placement" of the child as part of the "identification process." Under Pub. L. 94-142 this has few procedural safeguards other than notice to the parent when it begins, and parental consent is not required. The obvious abuse that must be guarded against is leaving the child there indefinitely. Some schools seem to find this appealing because they can deliver some level of services to the child but not be bothered with the individual plan. I have visited schools where children are kept for several years in such "diagnostic placements." Sham practices such as these will undoubtedly be litigated against on the grounds that there were no procedural safeguards, it was needlessly restrictive, and the level of services offered was inadequate. Any school that attempts to use diagnostic placements should tightly control the practice and be ready to move to evaluation and the individual education plan within a stipulated short period of time.

Placements in institutions

Another area of great flux is the use of institutionalization as the final step in the continuum of services available. A recent case, *Halderman v. Pennhurst*, found that institutions for the retarded were inherently unconstitutional because they are too restrictive. They isolate individuals away from the nonhandicapped and subject them to group regimens that are counter-rehabilitative. The 72 page opinion thoroughly demolished institutions as an acceptable alternative so that in the near future schools may be barred from making such a recommendation.

8 Procedural Safeguards

Testimony to Congress and in several court cases indicated that parents were often left out of decisions about special education for their children. Further, notice, when given, was often incomprehensible or intimidating, it often came after the fact, and it elicited acquiescence but seldom consent. All that has been changed under Pub. L. 94-142 and Section 504.

Prior notice necessary

Notice is now required to be given before any step is taken in regard to the child. 45 CFR 121a.504(a)(1)-(2) requires written notice "a reasonable time before the public agency proposes to initiate or change (or refuses to initiate or change) the identification, evaluation or placement of the child or the provision of a free appropriate public education to the child."

This means that at each step the school must tell the parents whether it plans to go ahead. It recognizes that it is important to tell the parents when services are proposed, but equally important to tell the parents when the school is no longer planning to provide services. Thus, parents will be alerted at the earliest possible time whether they want to argue that services should be begun, continued, or terminated.

In a typical case, notice might be required at least five times the first year. First, when the school proposes to identify the child through normal screening techniques such as teacher observation or gathering of existing data, it must notify the parent that such screening is to be done. Second, when the results of the identification process are known, the school would notify the parent that they will do no more, or that they propose to move to the evaluation process. Third, once the evaluation is completed, the school must notify the parent that nothing more will be done, or that they are scheduling an individual education planning meeting. Fourth, after the individual education planning meeting, the school must notify the parents of the proposed educational placement. And fifth, at the end of the year, the school must notify the parent that the annual review of progress will be held. At each step, if the parents disagree, they have a right to go to an impartial due process hearing.

Notice must be comprehensible

The notice must be written at a general level of comprehension—"language understandable to the general public"—and in the native language of the parent. Where the parent cannot communicate in a written language the notice must be translated orally or by other means. This means that the school must be prepared to offer notice in foreign languages, sign language, or in any other way to accommodate the parent. (As noted in Chapter 6, at the individual education planning conference interpreters must be made available if needed by the parents.)

Where the notice was given in other than a written language, the school must document that notice was given in this alternative mode and that "the parent understands the content of the notice" [45 CFR 121a.505(c)(2)-(3)].

Procedural safeguards required in general notice

The federal law addresses the content of the notice in a general requirement that there be "a full explanation of all the procedural safeguards available to the parents under Subpart E" and then requires notice specific to the proposed actions. The Subpart E regulations (45 CFR 121a) would include at least the following categories of information:

1. Records: Right to inspect and review records; right to make copies of records; right to receive a list of all types and locations of records being collected, maintained, or used by the agency; right to ask for an explanation of any

item in the records; right to ask for an amendment of any record on the grounds it is inaccurate, misleading, or violates privacy rights; right to a hearing on the issue if the agency refuses to make the amendment.

2. Independent evaluation: Right to an independent educational evaluation; right to be told where an independent evaluation may be obtained at no expense or low expense; right to have the agency pay for the evaluation if the agency's evaluation was not appropriate; right to be told that an impartial hearing officer may be asked to order an independent evaluation at public expense; right to be told the criteria for the evaluation examiner needed to secure payment by the agency.

3. Notice: Right to notice before the agency initiates or changes, or refuses to initiate or change, the identification, evaluation, or placement of the child; right to have that notice in writing in the parents' native language or other principal mode of communication, at a level understandable to the general public; right to have the notice describe the proposed action, explain why it is proposed, describe the options considered and explain why the other options were rejected; right to be notified of each evaluation procedure, test, record, or report the agency will use as a basis for any proposed action.

4. Consent: Right to consent before an evaluation is conducted and before initial placement in special education; right to revoke consent at any time; right of agency to proceed in the absence of consent to a hearing to determine if the child should be initially evaluated or initially placed; right of parent to protest at a hearing such an action in the absence of consent.

5. Hearing: Right of parent to request an impartial due process hearing to question the agency's identification, evaluation, placement of a child, or provision of a free appropriate public education; right to be told of any free or low-cost legal and other relevant services available (e.g., an expert on handicapped conditions that may be a witness at the hearing); right to have the hearing chaired by a person

not employed by a public agency involved in education of the child or otherwise having any personal or professional interest in the hearing; right to see a statement of the qualifications of the hearing officer; right to be accompanied to the hearing and advised by counsel and individuals with special knowledge or training in problems of the handicapped; right to have the child present; right to have the hearing open to the public; right to present evidence and confront, cross-examine and compel the attendance of witnesses; right to prohibit the introduction at the hearing of any evidence that has not been disclosed at least five days before the hearing; right to have a record of the hearing; right to obtain written findings of fact and a written decision within 45 days after the agency received the initial request for the hearing; right to appeal to the state educational agency and receive a decision within 30 days of the filing of an appeal; right to have a hearing and appeal which allows oral arguments, to be set at a time reasonably convenient to the parent; right to appeal a decision from the state educational agency into court; right to have the child remain in his present educational placement during the pendency of the administrative proceeding, unless parent and agency agree otherwise.

6. Surrogate parent: Responsibility of agency to appoint a surrogate parent when no one can be identified as acting in the place of a parent.

7. Evaluation procedures: Right to have a full and individual evaluation of the child's educational needs; right to be assured that testing does not discriminate on the basis of language or culture; right to have tests sensitive to impaired sensory, manual, or speaking skills; right to have more than one criterion used in determining the appropriate educational program; right to have the evaluation performed by a multidisciplinary team; right to have the child assessed in all areas related to the suspected disability; right to have a reevaluation every three years or more frequently if conditions warrant or if the child's parent or teacher requests it.

8. Least restrictive environment: Right to have children educated with nonhandicapped children to the maximum extent appropriate; right to have handicapped children removed from the regular educational environment only after supplementary aids and services were tried and found unsatisfactory; right to have a continuum of alternative placements so that removal from the regular educational environment can be the least necessary deviation; right to have supplementary services such as a resource room or itinerant instruction to make it possible to remain in regular class placement; right to have placement in the school the child would attend if nonhandicapped unless the individual education plan requires some other arrangement; right of the child to participate with the nonhandicapped in nonacademic and extracurricular services and activities such as meals, recess, counseling, clubs, athletics, and special interest groups.

9. Confidentiality of information: Right to restrict access to your child's records by withholding consent to disclose records; right to be informed before information in the child's file is to be destroyed; right to be told to whom information has been disclosed.

Most schools are preparing booklets which discuss the above categories of information and are sending them to parents at the beginning of the school year.

Specific notice of proposed actions

In addition to the generalized notice described above, the specific action proposed must be detailed:

(1) The proposed action must be stated.

(2) There must be an explanation why the school proposes the action.

(3) A description must be given of the alternatives which were considered before the proposed action was decided on.

(4) The reasons must be explained why the other alternatives were rejected.

(5) Each evaluation procedure, test, record, or report that the

agency will rely on as a basis for the proposed action must be described.

(6) Any other factors relevant to the agency's proposed action must be described. [45 CFR 121a.505(a)(1)-(4)]

When consent is required

Notice and consent are often mentioned together as procedural safeguards, but consent need not be obtained for every step for which notice must be given. Consent is specifically required for only four things: (1) the initial evaluation of the child, (2) the initial placement of the child, (3) evaluation before a "subsequent significant change in placement," and (4) before release of records to persons not already authorized to see them.

Consent is not required for: (1) the identification process, (2) scheduled reevaluations, such as the triannual required evaluation, (3) simple changes in placement, or (4) the individual education program plan (so long as the child has previously been placed and is receiving special education services).

Who gives consent?

Who gives the consent, when it is required, is a controversial question. Pub. L. 94-142 uses the term "parent" and defines parent as a parent, guardian, person acting as a parent or an appointed surrogate. The term expressly excludes the state if the child is a ward of the state so that the state could not both propose a service and consent to it.

Recent court action suggests that the simple consent of a parent, in the face of open opposition by the child, may not be enough. In *Bartley v. Kremens* and *J. L. v. Parham*, two federal courts have required an opportunity for hearing when parents consented to place youths, over their protest, in institutions. Thus, there is uncertainty on these issues. First, there is some question where to draw the line on the constitutionally protected liberty interests. Inclusion in a regular classroom with a modified curriculum presumably would not raise the issue, but placement in an institution far from home probably would. A line must be drawn somewhere in between.

Second, when does the protected interest begin? Notice and an opportunity for a hearing to stop the whole process before it errs are there for the parents at the early stages of identification, evaluation, and program planning, as well as at the time of a placement. The Congress felt that even these small steps were important to protect. So what weight should a handicapped child's protest have at these early stages?

Third, would more weight be accorded the child's protest if the adult consenting is not the parent but is only acting as a parent or has been appointed to play that role as a surrogate? Presumably more weight would be given to the child's protest: (a) the closer the decision making gets to a placement, (b) the more restrictive the placement recommended, and (c) when the consenting party is not the actual parent.

Proceeding without parental consent

When consent is required in a proposed evaluation or placement and the parent refuses, state law determines if the agency must stop at that point. An underlying theme of both Section 504 and Pub. L. 94-142 is that the handicapped child is to be served. The parent cannot be allowed to block needed services any more than the school can be allowed to offer inadequate services. 45 CFR 121a.504(c) provides:

> (1) Where State law requires parental consent before a handicapped child is evaluated or initially provided special education and related services, State procedures govern the public agency in overriding a parent's refusal to consent.
>
> (2) (i) Where there is no State law requiring consent before a handicapped child is evaluated or initially provided special education and related services, the public agency may use the hearing procedures in sections 121a.506-508 to determine if the child may be evaluated or initially provided special education and related services without parental consent.
>
> (ii) If the hearing officer upholds the agency, the agency may evaluate or initially provide special education and related services to the child without the parent's consent, subject to the parent's rights under sections 121a.510-513. [Note: The latter sections guarantee the parent the right to an administrative appeal of the

hearing officer's decision and the right to contest it further in court.]

Federal law usually supersedes state law in the same subject area. Here, however, the federal law specifically provides for state law to control. If state law requires, for example, that the school obtain a court order to authorize conducting an evaluation over the parent's protest, then that law would prevail.

It is surprising, however, how many states do not have state laws on this issue. They may have a traditional practice—many local school boards have a policy that they stop as soon as the parent protests. But in the absence of explicit law at the state level, the federal provisions would prevail.

It is important to note that the federal regulations underscore what was noted earlier—that consent is required for initial evaluation and provision of services but not thereafter. Other than for these two times, federal regulations prohibit conditioning services on consent. 45 CFR 121a.504(b)(2) provides "Except for preplacement evaluation and initial placement, consent may not be required as a condition of any benefit to the parent or child." Thus, a school cannot require consent to an individual education plan and, upon failing to receive it, refuse to provide special education services. Some schools, unfortunately, have been doing that. The federal law requires that local schools bring their board policies into compliance with Pub. L. 94-142 so board policies that contradict this must be changed. Thus after services are being provided, the school is obligated to keep going, even over a parent's protest, with the parent, of course, being informed of the right to translate that protest into a request for an impartial hearing.

In the absence of state law, the federal law merely says that the school "may" use the hearing procedures. They do not have to. Therefore a school district must develop procedures to determine when and if they would go over a parent's protest to an impartial hearing. One would assume that, if an evaluation team felt strongly about recommending a placement, it would feel strongly enough to take that recommendation to a hearing should the parents refuse consent.

Should a school go to a hearing?

There are two items the school would want to weigh in determining whether or not to go to a hearing. First, what is there to lose for the child? Would forcing the services over the protest of an irate parent really serve the child? In some instances the need would be great enough; in others, perhaps not. What would be lost at home and the impact that loss would have on the overall program are surely of concern to the school.

Second, what does the school have to lose? Many school personnel have considered the following scenario: A 13-year-old child needs services for a learning disability. The parents refuse and the school keeps the child in the regular classroom where he does poorly. He develops an erratic attendance record, is occasionally suspended, and gets a juvenile record. He drops out of school at the legal age but cannot read well enough for employment. At age 18 he has the right to see his school records, sees that the school felt he needed special help but never gave it, and sues. It might happen. If the school felt sure enough about the need for services to recommend them at one time but then just let the matter drop, even though they had the procedure by which they could have gone over the parent's protest and delivered the services, then the school might be liable. A school should never make a casual recommendation for evaluation or placement on which they are not willing to follow through.

Surrogate parents

Under Pub. L. 94-142 the involvement of a parent to protect the interests of the child is very important. It is inconceivable that there would not be someone there to receive the notice, provide needed consent, participate in the annual program planning conference, and call for an impartial hearing if something goes wrong. Thus, if there is not a parent, a surrogate parent must be appointed to protect the child's interests under 45 CFR 121a.514.

"Parent" is defined at 45 CFR 121a.10 as "a parent, guardian, a person acting as a parent of a child, or a surrogate parent who has been appointed in accordance with section

121a.514. The term does not include the State if the child is a ward of the State."

Section 121a.514 requires the appointment of a surrogate parent under any of the following conditions. First, a surrogate is needed if "no parent can be identified." Parent is defined so broadly that if no parent can be identified, the child is probably not in the care of anyone over the age of 18.

Second, a surrogate is needed if the "public agency, after reasonable efforts, cannot discover the whereabouts of a parent." In this alternative, someone presumably exists as a parent but is just not there to receive notice or participate in meetings.

In either of the above, a school would presumably face other requirements upon discovery that a handicapped student is virtually alone or abandoned. Through some social services mechanism aid would be found which might include the appointment of a guardian or placement of the child with someone who could then meet the definition of parent.

Third, a surrogate is needed "if the child is a ward of the State under the laws of that State." The fear here was the practice of the superintendent of a facility being appointed guardian for all wards in the program and then being in a position of offering a program as a service provider and consenting to it as guardian. The potential for abuse is too great. Thus in the final regulations, as explained at 42 Fed. Reg. 42512 (Aug. 23, 1977), no employee of any agency involved in education or care of the child can serve as the surrogate parent. (The fact that a surrogate is paid by the agency to serve as a surrogate does not mean that the surrogate is an employee.) If the child is a ward, a surrogate is needed.

The agency's duty is to determine whether a specific child needs a surrogate and, if so, to assign one to the child. In choosing the surrogate, the agency must insure that the person selected "has no interest that conflicts with the interests of the child he or she represents," and further that the surrogate "has knowledge and skills that insure adequate representation of the child" [45 CFR 121a.514(c)(2)]. Requirements for personnel development [45 CFR 121a.382(f)(3) and 383(c)] establish that it is the school's responsibility for the training of the surrogate parent, if it is needed. Thus, the school must train surrogates to "insure" they have adequate "knowledge and skills."

The appointment of a surrogate is considered a very serious step. Schools should consider developing a policy to seek judicial ratification of their choice. Many persons question whether parents or students might later sue a surrogate for somehow damaging their interests. In explanatory comments at 42 Fed. Reg. 42512 (Aug. 23, 1977) the regulations state: "The legal liability of surrogates will be determined under State law relating to such matters as breach of fiduciary duty, negligence and conflict of interest. The Federal Government has no authority to limit legal liability."

Reasons for requesting a hearing

A hearing may be requested in regard to notice, proposals to initiate or change (or refusal to initiate or change) identification, evaluation or educational placement, or the provision of a free appropriate public education. This appears to include every conceivable topic, so virtually any parental complaint would meet the test of being substantively within the purview of a due process hearing.

Delaying access to hearings

Many schools appear to be attempting to deny or delay access to hearings. Some local school regulations provide that parents must request a hearing within 15 days of the action about which they are complaining. Such schools are obviously trying to make it easier on themselves by imposing a technicality that will stifle requests and convince parents that the new right to an impartial hearing is really going to get them nothing.

Such timelines are meaningless within the protection of Pub. L. 94-142. For example, if the parents receive notice of a placement on September 1, and do nothing until September 16, then under the 15 day limit suggested by some schools they could no longer complain. However, on September 16 the parents can simply ask for a change in that placement and, when the school refuses, can request a hearing based not on the placement 16 days ago but on the refusal today. Parents can ask for a change at any time. If they do not get it, then they can ask for a hearing. Thus, short procedural timelines are not enforceable and schools should abandon them.

Another way in which many schools are attempting to delay access to a hearing is by requiring that the parent first go through already established grievance procedures. Typically a parent would have a meeting with the principal, then a special education supervisor, then the superintendent, then the school board, and possibly others. Requiring these procedures before allowing the parent access to an impartial hearing under Pub. L. 94-142 is in direct conflict with that law. In some states it would mean at least a full school year could be lost on local "remedies" before going into a hearing. That is not the intent of the new federal law. Comments in the regulations address this point at 42 Fed. Reg. 42495 (Aug. 23, 1977).

> Many states have pointed to the success of using mediation as an intervening step prior to conducting a formal due process hearing. Although the process of mediation is not required by the statute or these regulations, an agency may wish to suggest mediation in disputes concerning the identification, evaluation and educational placement of handicapped children, and the provision of a free appropriate public education to those children. Mediations have been conducted by members of State educational agencies or local educational agency personnel who were not previously involved in the particular case. In many cases, mediation leads to resolution of differences between parents and agencies without the development of an adversarial relationship and with minimal emotional stress. However, mediation may not be used to deny or delay a parent's rights under this subpart.

Parents have a right to have a final decision within 45 days from the time the school receives the request for a hearing. But the hearing officer may grant specific extensions of time beyond the 45 days. Therefore, it appears that the following procedure would be acceptable under the law. (1) The parent requests a hearing. (2) The school begins the 45 day time limit, but requests the parents to attend a mediation meeting. (3) The parents do so and, as things look promising for a solution, they ask the hearing officer for an extension of time. (4) However, if things turn sour, the parents can call off the mediation, notify the hearing officer, and the 45 day timeline begins again.

Mediation as an alternative to a hearing

There are two reasons why mediation is a workable alternative to a full impartial hearing. First, many parents who complain to schools are not taken seriously. No one in authority will listen to them. But with the threat of an impartial hearing, a mediator will suddenly listen. Some percentage of the complaints will be found to be reasonable and mediation will work because someone finally paid attention. Second, in many meetings in which the school does not agree with the parents' complaint there is no incentive for schools to bend over backwards. But under the threat of a full impartial hearing if the mediation fails, the school will make extra efforts to work out something reasonable. 45 CFR 84.7(b) requires each agency to have a Grievance Coordinator available to process complaints. The impartial Grievance Coordinator could be a mediator.

Thus, mediation can be an adjunct to the impartial hearing, not a stumbling block. It can be suggested by the schools, but it cannot be required as a precondition. Parents now have a right to a hearing; they do not have to earn that right by working through the school's idea of a hearing procedure.

Upon requesting a hearing, the parents must be informed of "any free or low-cost legal and other relevant services available in the area" [45 CFR 121a.506(c)]. Parents do not have to have a lawyer to go to a hearing but, as discussed above, the school may use some technicalities to give the parents the idea that they cannot have a hearing. Thus, access to a lawyer might be needed before a hearing, at the hearing, and afterwards in considering an appeal.

State hearings

The hearing is conducted by the local agency directly responsible for the education of the child unless state policy provides for the state to conduct the hearing. Many states have written into their annual program plan the provision that hearings will be held at the state level. Two problems have already become apparent in states that have chosen that route. The first is the burden on parents to travel to the state capitol for their initial hearing. That could mean greatly increased expense if they are accompanied by an attorney or expert witness, travel for a day, stay overnight, and so forth. It would be a needless expense for the local education agency personnel to make that same trip. The state would do better to send its hearing officer to the local site of the complaint. 45 CFR 121a.512(d) provides that if oral testimony is to be offered by the parents, the hearing "must be conducted at a time and place which is reasonably convenient to the parents and child involved." But the burden should not be on parents to demonstrate inconvenience and fight the state on a procedural matter even before the hearing is held.

A second problem has to do with confusion over 45 CFR 121a.507(a) and 510(b). The first provides that the person conducting the hearing will not be an employee of the public agency. The latter contemplates a state review of a hearing at the local level. This has been confused in some states with the state education agency interpretation that they can hold the initial hearing and that it can be chaired by a state education agency employee. The law is clear, however, that whoever conducts the initial hearing must not be an employee of the state agency.

Impartial hearing officer

In most cases the hearings will be conducted at the local agency level. That hearing must be chaired by an impartial due process hearing officer, which is defined as: (1) a person not employed by any public agency involved in the education or care of the child, and (2) a person who does not have a personal or professional interest which would conflict with his or her objectivity in the hearing. Both aspects of this definition are important. Many schools apparently overlooked the second qualification and picked school board members as hearing officers since they are not "employees." That clearly would not meet the second qualification since the board members are responsible for the program or process being complained about. In recognition of this, a "comment" in the regulations specifically disqualifies school board members. Some schools have suggested using school board members from neighboring school districts as a way around that disqualification. That would still be susceptible to challenge because what school board member would make a costly ruling in a neighboring district and not expect to have to follow it in his own? Again, this would conflict with objectivity.

Some states are using hearing panels and that is permissible under the statute. In one state the school picks a person, the parent picks a second, and together they pick a third. This has some appealing advantages, but there are two disadvantages. First, hearing officers must be trained. There is always the possibility that the parent's choice and the joint choice may be new to the system, thus causing constant training needs. Second, since hearing officers will presumably be paid (and payment does not disqualify them as "employees"), the panel would triple the costs.

Some states are using attorneys as hearing officers and some are using special education professionals from local institutions of higher education. Hopefully all states will attempt to learn from each other and select and train good hearing officers. That would definitely serve both sides' interests.

Whoever is chosen, the agency must keep a list of the persons who serve as hearing officers. "The list must include a statement of the qualifications of each of those persons" [45 CFR 121a.507(c)]. One can infer from that provision that qualifications are a legitimate issue on which to challenge the selection of a hearing officer and further that qualifications would be an issue that could be raised on appeal. The regulation does not specifically state that the parent may see the list of hearing officers, but it would certainly be an implied right. An organization concerned with handicapped citizens might want to inspect the list in general and oppose it as biased. And a specific parent might want to inspect the qualifications of the hearing officer selected to hear that parent's case.

Scheduling a hearing
When parents request a hearing it must be scheduled at a time and place reasonably convenient to the parents and child if

the parents plan to present oral testimony. If the local agency is holding the hearing that should not present a problem, but if the state holds the initial hearing it may cause a problem, as indicated above.

The parent has a right to a final written decision within 45 days of the request for a hearing. That maximum time limit is important, but it does not give any guidance on when to set the hearing. In *Hairston v. Drosick* the court required the hearing to be scheduled within 5 days of the receipt of the request for a hearing, and the date of the hearing must be at least 15 days from the date of scheduling. That assures promptness in getting the procedure underway and also provides time for each side to prepare their case. It would leave several weeks for the hearing to be held and a decision written, all within the 45 day limit.

Another case which discusses time limits, *Mills v. Board of Education,* requires the hearing to be scheduled no sooner than 20 days from the receipt of the request. That is to give the parents adequate notice and *Mills* indicates it is waivable by parents ready to proceed. The *Mills* decision was long before Pub. L. 94-142's 45 day limit was set. *Mills* allows the hearing officer 30 days to render a written decision which, of course, might be too long under Pub. L. 94-142.

Once things are scheduled, the hearing officer may grant specific extensions of time at the request of either party. For example, the school might want to perform a reevaluation, or the parent and school might have begun some mediation process that appears promising.

The parent has the right to appear at the hearing and be accompanied by legal counsel and "by persons with special knowledge or training with respect to the problems of handicapped children" [45 CFR 121a.508(a)(1)]. The parent must bear the expense for such representation but, as mentioned above, the parent has the right to be told where he can obtain "free or low-cost legal and other relevant services."

The child also has a right to attend the hearing. *Hairston v. Drosick,* the only case to mention the issue, requires that "the child have the right to determine whether or not the child will attend the hearing." Depending on the age and disability of the child, Pub. L. 94-142 sees the parent as helping the child make that decision. Parents also have the right to open a hearing to the public. Since information to be discussed is confidential (see Chapter 9), parents could restrict the audience if they chose.

Presenting evidence in a hearing

At the hearing both parties have the right to present evidence. Both parties have the right to prohibit the introduction into evidence of anything not disclosed to them at least 5 days before the hearing. This concept of "discovery" is very important in the proceedings. The purpose of hearings will not be served by surprise. Similarly, earlier efforts at mediation cannot be served by any party withholding information. If both parties share the evidence they are relying upon at least 5 days before the hearing, some disputes might be settled in advance.

Both parties have the right to compel attendance of witnesses and confront and cross-examine them. Two problems arise. First, how is compulsory attendance to be carried out? Some schools' guidelines say the school will "request" an individual to appear. The statute requires them to "compel" attendance [20 U.S.C. 1415(d)(2)]. There is a big difference. Assume that a parent wants the school psychologist, who tested the child the previous year and caused her to be placed in a "trainables" program, to appear. But the psychologist is no longer working with the school and now lives in another city. What authority is there to force him to appear? The regulations offer little explanation. If the hearing were held at the state level, then the state Administrative Procedure Act might give the state educational agency subpoena power. But at the local level this authority is unclear.

The other problem with the compelled attendance of witnesses, assuming some "compelled" witnesses will not appear, is the evidentiary problems this creates. Assume that the psychologist described above does not appear. If the parent then has no one to "confront and cross-examine" with regard to the test in question, could the parent move to prohibit the introduction of the evidence that individual would have testified about? As noted in *Hairston v. Drosick* the decision must be based solely upon the evidence and testimony presented at the hearing, so the absence of a witness could prove decisive.

Schools will have to develop policies to deal with these contingencies. The idea is not to make the school's job impossible, but to allow the parents a fair opportunity to inquire into the school's decision-making process. Many schools feel that the whole hearing process is a game set up to "get the school." A comment in the proposed regulations at 41 Fed. Reg. 56972 (Dec. 30, 1976) addresses this fear:

> Many commenters have expressed concerns (a) that local educational agencies are totally vulnerable in any due process hearing and (b) that the entire process works only to the advantage of the individual handicapped child or his parents regardless of what the subject or purpose of the hearing may be. The Department's view with respect to this concern is as follows:
>
> A basic tenet of the American system of government, as provided by the United States Constitution, is that any individual who is threatened or becomes subject to serious or adverse action by public authorities must be provided with full rights of due process of law. Such procedures provide to the individual the opportunity to contest the proposed action within a series of proceedings which insure that fairness and good judgment govern the entire decision-making process.
>
> The implementation of these procedures, however, must not be misunderstood by public educators, handicapped children, their families or advocates. They are not intended to give an advantage to any "side" in the decision-making process. Rather they are to produce a setting in which the interested parties understand the nature of a child, his needs, the procedures and process used to obtain that information, the proposed plan to meet the needs of the child, the review procedures to determine program effectiveness, and finally, their rights under the law. Invoking due process procedures does not inherently create adversary settings. The goal of the process is better programming for children, with better understanding of all parties—parents, children, educators and advocates, of their responsibilities, and a forum for continuous review.

Parents have a right to obtain a written or electronic verbatim record of the hearings. The parents also have the right to appeal and obtain a decision within 30 days so the school would have to provide the record of the lower hearing very quickly. The copy should be free. Copies of the child's school records are provided at cost, but schools should not attempt to charge for the hearing record. A comment published at 42 Fed. Reg. 42511 (Aug. 23, 1977) suggests that the only costs the parents will bear are for their representatives and witnesses. Another comment at 42 Fed. Reg. 42512 (Aug. 23, 1977) states "it is expected that a copy of any decision would be provided to the parent at no cost."

Along with the written decision mailed to both parties, they receive written "findings of fact." These are important because they indicate upon what the hearing officer based his decision. Both parties should scrutinize the findings of fact to make sure they are accurately stated. The decision must obviously square with the facts as stated, and the facts must be directly traceable to evidence contained in the record of the hearing. A problem discovered in one state was that hearing officers were assuming their personal experiences to be generally accepted. For example, a hearing officer who was a speech pathologist would rely on his own personal experiences in dealing with the type of child in the hearing. The hearing officer would then base his opinion on facts from his own knowledge which were not presented in the hearing.

Summary of notice and hearing requirements

The decision in *Hairston v. Drosick* explained very well the notice and hearing procedures and offers a good summary:

> Providing for a hearing in the event that the conference with the parents does not result in an agreement as to the placement of the children including: a fifteen day written notice; assurances that the child will remain in the present educational placement until a decision is entered following the hearing; granting the parents the opportunity to obtain evaluation of the child's educational needs and giving the parents access to school reports, files and records pertaining to the child for inspection and copying at reasonable cost; the right to request the attendance at the hearing of any employee or agent of the county educational agency who

might have testimony or evidence relative to the needs, abilities, or status of the child; the scheduling of the hearing within five days of the request and that the county board of education supply to the parents written notice of the time and place within at least fifteen days prior to the hearing; a verbatim record or tape recording of the proceedings to be provided by the county.

That the hearing be presided over by an impartial hearing officer; that the parties have an opportunity to present their evidence and testimony; that the hearing shall be closed to the public unless the parents request an open hearing; that the parents and other persons have an opportunity to confront and question all witnesses at the hearing; that the child have the right to determine whether or not the child will attend the hearing; that the burden of proof as to the appropriateness of any proposed placement be upon the school personnel recommending the placement; that a decision be issued within thirty days of the decision in writing and forwarded by certified mail to the parents; that the decision include findings of fact, conclusions, and reasons for these findings and conclusions; that such decision be based solely upon the evidence and testimony presented at the hearing; and that the parents be afforded a mechanism for administrative appeal.

Appeals

The "mechanism for administrative appeal" applies to the state education agency if the local agency held the initial hearing. After the state level appeal (or after the state level hearing if the impartial due process hearing was held initially at the state level) either party may appeal to state or federal court.

The decision of the original hearing officer is final unless appealed. Some schools are making the mistake of setting up procedures for hearings to be automatically referred to the local school board. That is acceptable if the local school board is simply determining if it wants to appeal an adverse decision. But it is not acceptable to have a system that does not enforce the hearing officer's decision until the board votes to accept it. The school board must enforce the decision or appeal it.

At the appellate level, the state reviewing official has a great deal of discretion and a broad scope of review. He can seek additional evidence "if necessary." He can give the parties an opportunity to make oral or written arguments at his own discretion. He then examines the entire record from the hearing plus any new evidence he has allowed to be presented. He also reviews the procedures at the initial hearing to assure they met due process requirements.

The reviewing official then makes a written decision within 30 days of the receipt of the request for a review and mails the decision to both parties. That decision is final unless appealed into state or federal courts. The state level reviewing official must meet the same minimum standard of impartiality required of the impartial hearing officer (i.e., not an agency employee nor someone with a professional or personal interest that would affect objectivity) (1975 U.S. Code Cong. and Ad. News, p. 1502).

If the appeal is appealed into court, the court shall receive the records of the administrative proceedings and hear additional evidence "at the request of a party" [Pub. L. 94-142, § 615(e)(2)]. In making its ruling the court will use the standard of proof known as the "preponderance of the evidence." The regulations do not address the standard of proof required in the state agency review, but presumably the reviewing official would require the hearing officer's decision to be supported by a preponderance of the evidence.

Some states are attempting to limit parents' access to court by requiring that an appeal of the state reviewing official's decision is final unless appealed within a specific time, such as 10 days. Nothing in the statute gives the state agency the right to condition access to the court. Certainly if a lengthy delay were to occur, a court petitioned by the aggrieved party might rule adversely. But tight procedural limitations are simply attempts by state bodies to lessen their exposure; increase the burden on the parents; make it more likely that a parent, to succeed, must hire legal counsel; and generally frustrate the intent of this provision of the law.

Child's placement during a hearing

During the whole proceedings the child is intended to be served. If the child is already being served in some way, then he is to stay in that present educational placement unless the parents and the agency agree to place him elsewhere. If the complaint involves admission to school, the child "must be placed in the public school program until the completion of all the proceedings."

Decisions made in hearings are to be referred to the State Advisory Panel on the Education of Handicapped Children. The regulations do not detail what is to be done with that information other than that the Panel is to assist in developing and reporting such information as may assist the United States Commissioner of Education in measuring the impact of the overall program. It would be very helpful if the Panel were to report hearing and appeal decisions so that they could be viewed statewide. Parties thinking about arguing a certain matter at the hearing level who could see that the issue was not being sustained on appeal at the state level would presumably avoid needless waste of time, effort, and expense. Local schools could also see what school policies and practices were being struck down and which were being sustained statewide and could act accordingly. The Panel could view the kinds of complaints arising out of a specific district and advise the state office about apparent needs for reform. Thus, the results of hearings could be used to improve the overall system.

Hearing officers' training

For the hearing system to work, hearing officers must be trained and the regulations contemplate that this responsibility is to be borne by the schools. Schools' interests would not be served by unleashing untrained hearing officers whose rulings might be overturned, causing needless expenses and wasting the time of school personnel. The only hearing officer "training manuals" which I have seen do not really train an officer to conduct a hearing or to rule on predictable procedural problems. They focus rather on clerical detail that would turn the hearing officer into a clerk making extensive unregulated contact with the parties and amassing mountains of paper prior to the hearing.

Hearing officers ought to be trained to deal with hearings

in regard to at least the following 12 issues (obviously, several of these issues could overlap in one hearing):

1. adequacy of notice
2. identification, or failure to identify
3. evaluation, or failure to evaluate
4. appropriateness of placement
5. appropriateness of public offering and possible payment by school of outside placement
6. provision of related services
7. possible payment by school of costs being billed to parents
8. provision of services in the least restrictive alternative
9. payment by school of the cost of parent-obtained independent educational evaluation
10. continuation, at public expense, of private placement begun by parents
11. adequacy of parental consent
12. school's proceedings in obtaining an initial evaluation or initial placement in the absence of parental consent

A hearing officer must also be trained in: (1) ordering further evaluations; (2) compelling attendance of witnesses; (3) admitting, or prohibiting admission of, evidence; (4) reasons for which extensions of time might be granted prior to hearings; (5) reasons for which postponement might be ordered during a hearing; (6) which party has the burden of proof on an issue and will thus fail if it cannot be sustained; (7) writing "findings of fact" and the decision; (8) if there is an appeal, certifying the official record and transferring it to the state reviewing official; (9) making rulings during the hearing and noting those rulings, and parties' objections, for the record; and (10) procedure to respond before or during a hearing to the challenge that the hearing officer is unqualified or biased.

Prehearing procedures

Existing training manuals ignore prehearing procedures which could streamline the process and lead to fair and inexpensive hearings. A prehearing conference should be held to: (a) simplify issues, and eliminate those not relevant to a decision in the case; (b) gain agreement between parties as to certain facts and evidence to avoid the time consumed in introducing these through testimony; (c) explain the details of the procedures at the hearing to avoid later misunderstandings or emergency requests for postponements; (d) limit the number of witnesses to those necessary to establish the case, and discourage both parties from a parade of repetitious witnesses; (e) determine if any of the witnesses must be compelled to appear, if compelling such witnesses presents problems, and if some other witnesses can be satisfactorily substituted; and (f) if the evaluation of the child is one of the issues and the hearing officer agrees, order an evaluation so that at the hearing the parties may proceed rather than having to stop midway to obtain a satisfactory evaluation of the child.

Such a prehearing conference would not prejudice the hearing officer because no substantive issues would be explored. It certainly does not contravene anything in the statute and actually a prehearing conference could be considered part of the "mediation as an intervening step prior to conducting a formal due process hearing" [45 CFR 121a.506 Comment]. Such mediation is certainly to be encouraged and one could imagine some disputes being resolved at a prehearing conference.

9 Record Keeping and Confidentiality

A large number of court cases (see Rioux & Sandow, 1974) reveal that several abuses were common practice in schools. Parents were typically denied access to their child's records. In special education, the most important records, particularly any containing professional evaluations, were labeled "confidential." If parents did somehow obtain access and found a part of the record that they disagreed with, there was no process for amendment. And ironically, at the same time parents were being barred from seeing their child's records, everyone else in town was getting in there—from employment agencies and credit bureaus to law enforcement officials. These abuses were reported in the public press and were addressed in an amendment to Pub. L. 93-380, the Education Amendments of 1974. Regulations implementing the amendment were published at 41 Fed. Reg. 24670 (June 17, 1976). Those requirements are reiterated in the regulations under Pub. L. 94-142 and Section 504. Although they apply to all school children they are especially critical in regard to special education information.

As mentioned in Chapter 8's discussion of "notice," parents of handicapped children must be notified in writing of their right to have access to records, to amend those records, and to restrict others' access to them.

"Educational records"

The first question is what is an educational record? "Educational records means those records which: (1) are directly related to a student, and (2) are maintained by an educational agency or institution or by a party acting for the agency or institution" (45 CFR 99.3).

That answers one argument often raised by schools refusing access. The argument is that the school did not create the records, they came from a psychiatrist (or other outside source) and, therefore, the school has no right to show them to the parent. But a record is any personally identifiable information "maintained" by the school or by an individual consulting for the school. Anything the school has on a child is his "record."

Another argument is that the regulations provide for certain exceptions to parental access. One of these exceptions is "records of instructional, supervisory, and administrative personnel and educational personnel ancillary thereto which: are in the sole possession of the maker thereof, and are not accessible or revealed to any other individual except a substitute" [45 CFR 99]. The school might argue: "Our teacher (or other personnel) keeps certain records in her file so the parent cannot see them." But the type of special education information we are concerned with is revealed to other individuals. If it has an impact on the identification, evaluation, placement, or provision of a free appropriate public education then it played a role in a joint decision-making process. The fact that it is maintained separately from the student's file folder does not mean it has not been "revealed" in discussions and must therefore be considered part of the record.

A third argument revolves around another exception in the regulations. The definition of educational records does not apply to records which are: "(i) Created or maintained by a physician, psychiatrist, psychologist, or other recognized professional or paraprofessional acting in his or her professional or paraprofessional capacity, or assisting in that capacity; (ii) created, maintained, or used only in conjunction with the provision of treatment to the student, and (iii) not disclosed to anyone other than individuals providing the treatment; *Provided,* that the records can be personally reviewed by a physician or other appropriate professional of the student's choice. For the purpose of this definition, 'treatment' does not include remedial educational activities or activities which are part of the program of instruction at the educational agency or institution" [45 CFR 99]. Some schools read this to exclude records that were developed by psychiatrists or psychologists. Clearly that is not the case, for once these individuals disclose the information to any school person it becomes part of the educational record. The definition of the term "treatment" indicates that the exemption in this section does not apply to any part of the special education program, so any information relating to special education would be part of the record. Finally, even those records truly kept out of education and separate from all school personnel and school decision making can be examined by a professional of the student's choice.

Another argument cannot be answered so clearly. A battle is beginning in some parts of the country to obtain the test protocols used in administering tests to children. Because of the experience with cultural and racial bias in testing, knowledge of the questions asked is important. Parents will not be content with just being told a numerical score. Equally important, test protocols reflect specific universes of information (such as knowledge of a certain number of words at a certain level) that overlap with commercially prepared reading material. At the elementary level, a child who is taught to read in a certain prereading program will do well on a test which coincidentally depends on a similar universe of words. Unfortunately, a child who takes that test but has been using a different reading series may score dramatically lower. This can, and does, lead to misclassification. It is certainly important to be able to see the questions asked before simply accepting a test score.

But schools argue that test protocols are not part of the child's educational record. They are not "directly related to a student." Schools feel that they cannot release test protocols because of copyright protection. There are ethical constraints prohibiting persons from releasing test protocols; if parents disclosed test questions and answers it could destroy the validity of the tests, rendering them of no use to the school, casting doubt on test scores, and creating great expense in the selection and validation of new tests. Schools also argue that parents could not understand the test protocols anyway.

The issue cannot be clearly resolved here. The regulations do not really address it. However, *National Labor Relations Board v. Detroit Edison* seems analogous. In that case the company administered psychological aptitude tests and used the results to determine eligibility of employees for promotion. The union wanted to see the test protocols and answer sheets as well as just getting the scores. The company agreed only to turn the requested information over to a qualified psychologist who could then advise the union. The federal appeals court held that the union had a right to examine the protocols with the protection that they could not copy or disclose them and must return them to the company. The court felt that this would meet all the objections raised by the company, which were similar to the schools' concerns detailed above. Schools can expect that parents will increasingly view protocols as being as much a part of the record as the test scores and will demand access to them.

Right of access to records
Parents, and students over the age of 18, must have access to educational records. Virtually anything to be used by the school in regard to the child must be disclosed. This is only logical in light of the following two provisions of the law. When proposing to initiate or change, or refusing to initiate or change, services to a child, the school must notify the parent by describing "each evaluation procedure, test, record, or report the agency uses as a basis" [45 CFR 121a.505(a)(3)]. Similarly, if the school were to go to a hearing they would have to disclose, 5 days in advance, everything on which they were going to rely in the hearing. Those broad disclosure provisions underscore the full right of access to the records. Anything "collected, maintained or used by the agency" must be available for inspection and review.

Schools typically keep many files on a child with the relevant personnel keeping files in separate locations. When parents ask one of these persons to see their child's records, that person is likely to show them only what the person himself maintains. This leads to misunderstanding, frustration, and a feeling on the part of parents that they are being slighted. The parents have a right to request and receive a list of the types and locations of education records. When the parents then make an appointment to see the records it would be reasonable to ask that all the records be made available at one specified location.

When a parent makes a request to inspect the records it must be complied with without any unreasonable delay and in no case more than 45 days after the request. Some schools automatically schedule such requests for the 45th day, and should be susceptible to an attack that such a practice represents unreasonable delay.

There are two exceptions to the 45 day period for a school to respond. One is if the parent has asked for a hearing and the second is if the school has scheduled an individual education planning conference. In either case the parent must be given access before the hearing or the conference.

Right to explanations of records

Once the parents see the records, they have a right to make "reasonable requests for explanations and interpretations of the records" and the agency must respond [45 CFR 121a.562(b)(1)]. Some schools do not like to have parents see the records in private for fear that they will misunderstand something. Those schools use the above provision to suggest a need to have a school official on site at the time the parents review the file. Schools seem to feel this means that they are really meeting the right to a response for reasonable requests for explanations. Some parents, however, feel it is intimidating to have an official there. I have been told of some cases in which the official constantly commented about how busy he was, how he was being taken away from serving other children, and so forth, until the parent became intimidated and left the room. Schools should obviously see that their personnel do not act that way. It is probably best to let the parent review the file in private and respond to requests for explanations later.

Right to make copies of records

Parents have a right to make copies of records "if failure to provide those copies would effectively prevent the parent from

exercising the right to inspect and review the record" [45 CFR
121a.562(b)(2)]. There is no indication in the regulations how
this judgment is to be made or who has the burden of making it.
Suppose a parent said, "I can't read all of this and understand it.
I need to read and reread it on my own time. I also want to
show parts of it to an educator and to my lawyer so they can
help me understand it. Therefore, I want a copy." One could
not imagine that a school would respond, "We know that you can
effectively inspect the records here in one reading. Therefore,
we will not allow you to make copies." How could the school
ever prove its side of the issue? Yet every day many schools
refuse to make copies or otherwise attempt to discourage copies
from being made.

One major deterrent schools use against copying is cost.
This writer has been told of many different charges, ranging up
to 2 dollars per page. The agency may charge a fee for copies so
long as that fee does not "effectively prevent" the parents from
being able to inspect or review the records. No part of the fee
can be for searching out the requested information or retrieving
it. There is no standard for a fair cost per page. At 42 Fed. Reg.
42514 (Aug. 23, 1977) the Office of Education states: "Agencies may of course adopt policies of making copies available free
of charge and are encouraged to do so."

Right to amend records

Once the parents review the records, they may find some
portion with which they disagree. Parents who believe that information in the record is "inaccurate or misleading or violates
the privacy or other rights of the child, may request the participating agency which maintains the information to amend the
information" [45 CFR 121a.567(a)].

The school must decide, in a reasonable period of time,
whether to grant the request. If they decide not to amend the
record, they must notify the parents and also explain to the
parents their right to a hearing on the issue.

If the parents request such a hearing, the agency must
provide it within a reasonable time after receiving the request.
The hearing is not an "impartial due process hearing" as de-

scribed in Chapter 8. Its procedures are governed by provisions of the Family Educational Rights and Privacy Act, codified at 45 CFR 99.22.

The parents must be given notice of the date, place, and time of the hearing reasonably in advance of the hearing. The hearing may be conducted by any party (including an official of the school) so long as that party does not have a direct interest in the outcome of the hearing. The parents must have the opportunity to present evidence and be assisted or represented by individuals of their own choice, including an attorney. The school shall make its decision in writing within a reasonable time after the conclusion of the hearing. That decision shall be based solely on the evidence presented at the hearing and shall include a summary of the evidence and the reasons for the decision.

If the school's decision is not to amend the record, it must notify the parents of their right to place in the records a statement commenting on the information or setting forth reasons for disagreeing with the school's decision. That statement by the parents must be maintained by the school as part of the child's records as long as the contested portion is maintained. Further, if the contested portion of the record is shown to anyone, the parents' comment must also be shown to them.

Right to confidentiality of records

Disclosure of records with personally identifiable information to anyone other than parents or the parents' designated representatives must be closely controlled. Prior consent from parents for disclosure is not required: (1) for certain persons, such as the Commissioner of Education, defined at 45 CFR 99.31; (2) for school officials in a school to which the student is transferring; and (3) for officials within the child's current school "who have been determined by the agency or institution to have legitimate educational interests" [45 CFR 99].

In regard to the last category, the school must maintain, available for public inspection, a current listing of the names and positions of employees within the school who may have access to personally identifiable information. Thus, not everyone can have access. One official at each school shall be placed in charge of insuring confidentiality. All employees listed as having the right of access to children's records must receive training or instruction regarding state policies and procedures.

Before anyone else is given access to the records, parental consent must be obtained. That written consent must be signed and dated and must include: (1) a specification of the records to be disclosed, (2) the purpose of the disclosure, and (3) the party to whom the disclosure is to be made. A blanket permission for disclosure signed when the child enters the program would not be valid because the parent, at that time, would not be informed about the specific records disclosed, the purpose of the disclosure, or the party to whom disclosure will be made.

When access is given to the child's records (except access of the parents or designated school employees) the school must keep a record of those persons including their name, the date, and the purpose for which the party was authorized to use the records. When such a disclosure is made the parent has a right to request a copy of the exact portion of the record which was disclosed. Thus, the consent form by which a parent's permission is secured should contain the item: "Do you wish a copy of the portion of your child's record which is disclosed?"

One final exception to parental consent deals with health emergencies. This may be especially relevant to special education situations. If an emergency arises which is a serious threat to the health or safety of the child, specific information is needed to meet the emergency, the party to whom the information will be disclosed is in a position to deal with the emergency, and time is of the essence, then personally identifiable information may be disclosed.

Destroying information

Schools regularly destroy information as new evaluations make old information obsolete. Before a school destroys information that is personally identifiable, it must inform the parents that the information is no longer needed for educational planning. The school should inform the parents if some of the records it proposes to destroy might be needed by the parents later for social security benefits or other purposes. If the school no longer needs the information, and the parents request that it be destroyed, then it must be destroyed.

The school may permanently retain certain personally identifiable information such as a record of the student's name, address and phone number, grades, attendance record, classes attended, grade level completed, and year completed.

I have been told of the common practice of a school, upon receiving a request from the parents to review the child's records, looking at the folder and seeing something that should obviously be destroyed, and destroying it. This is an understandable response, but it is illegal. The Family Educational Rights and Privacy Act specifies that once a parent makes a request to see records, nothing may be changed or destroyed. Any questions about the complex provisions of this act can be addressed to the Family Educational Rights and Privacy Act Office, 330 Independence Avenue, S.W., Washington, D.C. 20201.

Afterword

Since the passage of the Education of the Handicapped Act, I have had the opportunity to work with personnel in over 100 programs for the handicapped in 25 states. I have also worked with parents of the handicapped in advocacy organizations in several states, occasionally aiding individual handicapped citizens. I am often told that I am overly optimistic and that one need only look at the country's lack of success in ending discrimination to realize that these new laws will not make a difference. I am told they demand too much and are unworkable.

I disagree. We needed these laws and regulations to make clearer exactly how the handicapped are being discriminated against. Most of our citizens and even some of the personnel working in programs for the handicapped do not understand what handicapped citizens face. The first step in making things better is for all of us to realize how bad we are making things now. I hope there will be a public outcry about these new regulations and questions about why we need to modify restrooms, what is reasonable accommodation in the performance of a job by a disabled person, why we need places for wheelchairs in theaters, and so forth. The debate over these issues will sensitize the public to all the facets of discrimination that currently exist. I am confident that most people will begin to understand these problems, be a little embarrassed at not having realized them before, and not oppose needed changes. I didn't say that the majority would demand change, but it is important that they no longer oppose others who want to work for change.

The second step will come as tangible barriers to participation of the handicapped are struck down. Our society is often told that the law cannot change people's minds. But the law *can* change the way people behave. Whenever a behavior physically exists, it can be dealt with. And whenever an individual's conduct erects a barrier, it can be removed. I am sure that consistently changed behavior will lead to a change in attitude after a period of years.

The third step toward making these laws work will come as our expectations change. I grew up in a racially segregated society. I never expected to see a black face in my schoolroom. My daughter now attends the same school I did and I expect her to have black schoolmates. I would be very suspicious if there were none because the law, and subsequent changes in overt behavior, have changed my expectations. When I was in school I was not sensitive to the denial of opportunity for girls to participate in many sports. The law has changed, my expectations have changed, and if my daughter wants to participate, I assume that the school will be ready to afford her the opportunity to participate. Our expectations will change with the handicapped. We will find it suspicious when our nonhandicapped children have no handicapped children in their classes and extracurricular activities.

So my optimism remains intact. I am confident that through the laws examined in this book we will see an end to the segregation that has kept the handicapped out of our schools. Whether we will then see the handicapped truly integrated into our society will be up to all of us.

Appendix
Excerpted Federal Regulations Governing Educational Services for Handicapped Children

Excerpts from Regulations under Public Law 93-112 Section 504 (All citations are to 45 Code of Federal Regulations and were published May 4, 1977, at 42 *Federal Register* 22676-22692.)

Subpart D—Preschool, Elementary, and Secondary Education

§ 84.31 **Application of this subpart.**

Subpart D applies to preschool, elementary, secondary, and adult education programs and activities that receive or benefit from federal financial assistance and to recipients that operate, or that receive or benefit from federal financial assistance for the operation of, such programs or activities.

§ 84.32 **Location and notification.**

A recipient that operates a public elementary or secondary education program shall annually:

(a) Undertake to identify and locate every qualified handicapped person residing in the recipient's jurisdiction who is not receiving a public education; and

(b) Take appropriate steps to notify handicapped persons and their parents or guardians of the recipient's duty under this subpart.

§ 84.33   Free appropriate public education.

(a) *General.* A recipient that operates a public elementary or secondary education program shall provide a free appropriate public education to each qualified handicapped person who is in the recipient's jurisdiction, regardless of the nature or severity of the person's handicap.

(b) *Appropriate education.* (1) For the purpose of this subpart, the provision of an appropriate education is the provision of regular or special education and related aids and services that (i) are designed to meet individual educational needs of handicapped persons as adequately as the needs of nonhandicapped persons are met and (ii) are based upon adherence to procedures that satisfy the requirements of § § 84.34, 84.35, and 84.36.

(2) Implementation of an individualized education program developed in accordance with the Education of the Handicapped Act is one means of meeting the standard established in paragraph (b) (1) (i) of this section.

(3) A recipient may place a handicapped person in or refer such person to a program other than the one that it operates as its means of carrying out the requirements of this subpart. If so, the recipient remains responsible for ensuring that the requirements of this subpart are met with respect to any handicapped person so placed or referred.

(c) *Free education–*(1) *General.* For the purpose of this section, the provision of a free education is the provision of educational and related services without cost to the handicapped person or to his or her parents or guardian, except for those fees that are imposed on nonhandicapped persons or their parents or guardian. It may consist either of the provision of free services or, if a recipient places a handicapped person in or refers such person to a program not operated by the recipient as its means of carrying out the requirements of this subpart, of payment for the costs of the program. Funds available from any public or private agency may be used to meet the requirements of this subpart. Nothing in this section shall be construed to relieve an insurer or similar third party from an otherwise valid obligation to provide or pay for services provided to a handicapped person.

(2) *Transportation.* If a recipient places a handicapped person in or refers such person to a program not operated by the recipient as its means of carrying out the requirements of this subpart, the recipient shall ensure that adequate transportation to and from the program is provided at no greater cost than would be incurred by the person or his or her parents or guardian if the person were placed in the program operated by the recipient.

(3) *Residential placement.* If placement in a public or private residential program is necessary to provide a free appropriate public education to a handicapped person because of his or her handicap, the program, including nonmedical care and room and board, shall be provided at no cost to the person or his or her parents or guardian.

(4) *Placement of handicapped persons by parents.* If a recipient has made available, in conformance with the requirements of this section and § 84.34, a free appropriate public education to a handicapped person and the person's parents or guardian choose to place the person in a private school, the recipient is not required to pay for the person's education in the private school. Disagreements between a parent or guardian and a recipient regarding whether the recipient has made such a program available or otherwise regarding the question of financial responsibility are subject to the due process procedures of § 84.36.

(d) *Compliance.* A recipient may not exclude any qualified handicapped person from a public elementary or secondary education after the effective date of this part. A recipient that is not, on the effective date of this regulation, in full compliance with the other requirements of the preceding paragraphs of this section shall meet such requirements at the earliest practicable time and in no event later than September 1, 1978.

§ 84.34   Educational setting.

(a) *Academic setting.* A recipient to which this subpart applies shall educate, or shall provide for the education of, each qualified handicapped person in its jurisdiction with persons who are not handicapped to the maximum extent appropriate to the needs of the handicapped person. A recipient shall place a handicapped person in the regular educational environment operated by the recipient unless it is demonstrated by the recipient that the education of the person in the regular environment with the use of supplementary aids and services cannot be achieved satisfactorily. Whenever a recipient places a person in a setting other than the regular educational environment pursuant to this paragraph, it shall take into account the proximity of the alternate setting to the person's home.

(b) *Nonacademic settings.* In providing or arranging for the provision of nonacademic and extracurricular services and activities, including meals, recess periods, and the services and activities set forth in § 84.37(a) (2), a recipient shall ensure that handicapped persons participate with nonhandicapped persons in such activities and services to the maximum extent appropriate to the needs of the handicapped person in question.

(c) *Comparable facilities.* If a recipient, in compliance with paragraph (a) of this section, operates a facility that is identifiable as being for handicapped persons, the recipient shall ensure that the facility and the services and activities provided therein are comparable to the other facilities, services, and activities of the recipient.

§ 84.35   Evaluation and placement.

(a) *Preplacement evaluation.* A recipient that operates a public elementary or secondary education program shall conduct an evaluation in accordance with the requirements of paragraph (b) of this section of any person who, because of handicap, needs or is believed to need special education or related services before taking any action with respect to the initial placement of the person in a regular or special education program and any subsequent significant change in placement.

(b) *Evaluation procedures.* A recipient to which this subpart applies shall establish standards and procedures for the evaluation and placement of persons who, because of handicap, need or are believed to need special education or related services which ensure that:

(1) Tests and other evaluation materials have been vali-

dated for the specific purpose for which they are used and are administered by trained personnel in conformance with the instructions provided by their producer;

(2) Tests and other evaluation materials include those tailored to assess specific areas of educational need and not merely those which are designed to provide a single general intelligence quotient; and

(3) Tests are selected and administered so as best to ensure that, when a test is administered to a student with impaired sensory, manual, or speaking skills, the test results accurately reflect the student's aptitude or achievement level or whatever other factor the test purports to measure, rather than reflecting the student's impaired sensory, manual, or speaking skills (except where those skills are the factors that the test purports to measure).

(c) *Placement procedures.* In interpreting evaluation data and in making placement decisions, a recipient shall (1) draw upon information from a variety of sources, including aptitude and achievement tests, teacher recommendations, physical condition, social or cultural background, and adaptive behavior, (2) establish procedures to ensure that information obtained from all such sources is documented and carefully considered, (3) ensure that the placement decision is made by a group of persons, including persons knowledgeable about the child, the meaning of the evaluation data, and the placement options, and (4) ensure that the placement decision is made in conformity with § 84.34.

(d) *Reevaluation.* A recipient to which this section applies shall establish procedures, in accordance with paragraph (b) of this section, for periodic reevaluation of students who have been provided special education and related services. A reevaluation procedure consistent with the Education for the Handicapped Act is one means of meeting this requirement.

§ 84.36 Procedural safeguards.

A recipient that operates a public elementary or secondary education program shall establish and implement, with respect to actions regarding the identification, evaluation, or educational placement of persons who, because of handicap, need or are believed to need special instruction or related services, a system of procedural safeguards that includes notice, an opportunity for the parents or guardian of the person to examine relevant records, an impartial hearing with opportunity for participation by the person's parents or guardian and representation by counsel, and a review procedure. Compliance with the procedural safeguards of section 615 of the Education of the Handicapped Act is one means of meeting this requirement.

§ 84.37 Nonacademic services.

(a) *General.* (1) A recipient to which this subpart applies shall provide nonacademic and extracurricular services and activities in such manner as is necessary to afford handicapped students an equal opportunity for participation in such services and activities.

(2) Nonacademic and extracurricular services and activities may include counseling services, physical recreational athletics, transportation, health services, recreational activities, special interest groups or clubs sponsored by the recipient, referrals to agencies which provide assistance to handicapped persons, and employment of students, including both employment by the recipient and assistance in making available outside employment.

(b) *Counseling services.* A recipient to which this subpart applies that provides personal, academic, or vocational counseling, guidance, or placement services to its students shall provide these services without discrimination on the basis of handicap. The recipient shall ensure that qualified handicapped students are not counseled toward more restrictive career objectives than are nonhandicapped students with similar interests and abilities.

(c) *Physical education and athletics.* (1) In providing physical education courses and athletics and similar programs and activities to any of its students, a recipient to which this subpart applies may not discriminate on the basis of handicap. A recipient that offers physical education courses or that operates or sponsors interscholastic, club, or intramural athletics shall provide to qualified handicapped students an equal opportunity for participation in these activities.

(2) A recipient may offer to·handicapped students physical education and athletic activities that are separate or different from those offered to nonhandicapped students only if separation or differentiation is consistent with the requirements of § 84.34 and only if no qualified handicapped student is denied the opportunity to compete for teams or to participate in courses that are not separate or different.

§ 84.38 Preschool and adult education programs.

A recipient to which this subpart applies that operates a preschool education or day care program or activity or an adult education program or activity may not, on the basis of handicap, exclude qualified handicapped persons from the program or activity and shall take into account the needs of such persons in determining the aid, benefits, or services to be provided under the program or activity.

§ 84.39 Private education programs.

(a) A recipient that operates a private elementary or secondary education program may not, on the basis of handicap, exclude a qualified handicapped person from such program if the person can, with minor adjustments, be provided an appropriate education, as defined in § 84.33(b) (1), within the recipient's program.

(b) A recipient to which this section applies may not charge more for the provision of an appropriate education to handicapped persons than to nonhandicapped persons except to the extent that any additional charge is justified by a substantial increase in cost to the recipient.

(c) A recipient to which this section applies that operates special education programs shall operate such programs in accordance with the provisions of § § 84.35 and 84.36. Each recipient to which this section applies is subject to the provisions of § § 84.34, 84.37, and 84.38.

Excerpts from Regulations under Public Law 94-142 (All citations are to 45 Code of Federal Regulations and were published August 23, 1977, at 42 *Federal Register* 42474-42514.)

§ 121a.5 Handicapped children.

(a) As used in this part, the term "handicapped children" means those children evaluated in accordance with § § 121a.530–121a.534 as being mentally retarded, hard of hearing, deaf, speech impaired, visually handicapped, seriously emotionally disturbed, orthopedically impaired, other health impaired, deaf-blind, multi-handicapped, or as having specific learning disabilities, who because of those impairments need special education and related services.

(b) The terms used in this definition are defined as follows:

(1) "Deaf" means a hearing impairment which is so severe that the child is impaired in processing linguistic information through hearing, with or without amplification, which adversely affects educational performance.

(2) "Deaf-blind" means concomitant hearing and visual impairments, the combination of which causes such severe communication and other developmental and educational problems that they cannot be accommodated in special education programs solely for deaf or blind children.

(3) "Hard of hearing" means a hearing impairment, whether permanent or fluctuating, which adversely affects a child's educational performance but which is not included under the definition of "deaf" in this section.

(4) "Mentally retarded" means significantly subaverage general intellectual functioning existing concurrently with deficits in adaptive behavior and manifested during the developmental period, which adversely affects a child's educational performance.

(5) "Multihandicapped" means concomitant impairments (such as mentally retarded-blind, mentally, retarded-orthopedically impaired, etc.), the combination of which causes such severe educational problems that they cannot be accommodated in special education programs solely for one of the

impairments. The term does not include deaf-blind children.

(6) "Orthopedically impaired" means a severe orthopedic impairment which adversely affects a child's educational performance. The term includes impairments caused by congenital anomaly (e.g., clubfoot, absence of some member, etc.), impairments caused by disease (e.g., poliomyelitis, bone tuberculosis, etc.), and impairments from other causes (e.g., cerebral palsy, amputations, and fractures or burns which cause contractures).

(7) "Other health impaired" means limited strength, vitality or alertness, due to chronic or acute health problems such as a heart condition, tuberculosis, rheumatic fever, nephritis, asthma, sickle cell anemia, hemophilia, epilepsy, lead poisoning, leukemia, or diabetes, which adversely affects a child's educational performance.

(8) "Seriously emotionally disturbed" is defined as follows:

(i) The term means a condition exhibiting one or more of the following characteristics over a long period of time and to a marked degree, which adversely affects educational performance:

(A) An inability to learn which cannot be explained by intellectual, sensory, or health factors;

(B) An inability to build or maintain satisfactory interpersonal relationships with peers and teachers;

(C) Inappropriate types of behavior or feelings under normal circumstances;

(D) A general pervasive mood of unhappiness or depression; or

(E) A tendency to develop physical symptoms or fears associated with personal or school problems.

(ii) The term includes children who are schizophrenic or autistic. The term does not include children who are socially maladjusted, unless it is determined that they are seriously emotionally disturbed.

(9) "Specific learning disability" means a disorder in one or more of the basic psychological processes involved in understanding or in using language, spoken or written, which may manifest itself in an imperfect ability to listen, think, speak,

read, write, spell, or to do mathematical calculations. The term includes such conditions as perceptual handicaps, brain injury, minimal brain dysfunction, dyslexia, and developmental aphasia. The term does not include children who have learning problems which are primarily the result of visual, hearing, or motor handicaps, of mental retardation, or of environmental, cultural, or economic disadvantage.

(10) "Speech impaired" means a communication disorder, such as stuttering, impaired articulation, a language impairment, or a voice impairment, which adversely affects a child's educational performance.

(11) "Visually handicapped" means a visual impairment which, even with correction, adversely affects a child's educational performance. The term includes both partially seeing and blind children.

§ 121a.13 Related services.

(a) As used in this part, the term "related services" means transportation and such developmental, corrective, and other supportive services as are required to assist a handicapped child to benefit from special education, and includes speech pathology and audiology, psychological services, physical and occupational therapy, recreation, early identification and assessment of disabilities in children, counseling services, and medical services for diagnostic or evaluation purposes. The term also includes school health services, social work services in schools, and parent counseling and training.

(b) The terms used in this definition are defined as follows:

(1) "Audiology" includes:

(i) Identification of children with hearing loss;

(ii) Determination of the range, nature, and degree of hearing loss, including referral for medical or other professional attention for the habilitation of hearing;

(iii) Provision of habilitative activities, such as language habilitation, auditory training, speech reading (lip-reading), hearing evaluation, and speech conservation;

(iv) Creation and administration of programs for prevention of hearing loss;

(v) Counseling and guidance of pupils, parents, and teachers regarding hearing loss; and

(vi) Determination of the child's need for group and individual amplification, selecting and fitting an appropriate aid, and evaluating the effectiveness of amplification.

(2) "Counseling services" means services provided by qualified social workers, psychologists, guidance counselors, or other qualified personnel.

(3) "Early identification" means the implementation of a formal plan for identifying a disability as early as possible in a child's life.

(4) "Medical services" means services provided by a licensed physician to determine a child's medically related handicapping condition which results in the child's need for special education and related services.

(5) "Occupational therapy" includes:

(i) Improving, developing or restoring functions impaired or lost through illness, injury, or deprivation;

(ii) Improving ability to perform tasks for independent functioning when functions are impaired or lost; and

(iii) Preventing, through early intervention, initial or further impairment or loss of function.

(6) "Parent counseling and training" means assisting parents in understanding the special needs of their child and providing parents with information about child development.

(7) "Physical therapy" means services provided by a qualified physical therapist.

(8) "Psychological services" include:

(i) Administering psychological and educational tests, and other assessment procedures;

(ii) Interpreting assessment results;

(iii) Obtaining, integrating, and interpreting information about child behavior and conditions relating to learning;

(iv) Consulting with other staff members in planning school programs to meet the special needs of children as indicated by psychological tests, interviews, and behavioral evaluations; and

(v) Planning and managing a program of psychological services, including psychological counseling for children and parents.

(9) "Recreation" includes:

(i) Assessment of leisure function;

(ii) Therapeutic recreation services;

(iii) Recreation programs in schools and community agencies; and

(iv) Leisure education.

(10) "School health services" means services provided by a qualified school nurse or other qualified person.

(11) "Social work services in schools" include:

(i) Preparing a social or developmental history on a handicapped child;

(ii) Group and individual counseling with the child and family;

(iii) Working with those problems in a child's living situation (home, school, and community) that affect the child's adjustment in school; and

(iv) Mobilizing school and community resources to enable the child to receive maximum benefit from his or her educational program.

(12) "Speech pathology" includes:

(i) Identification of children with speech or language disorders;

(ii) Diagnosis and appraisal of specific speech or language disorders;

(iii) Referral for medical or other professional attention necessary for the habilitation of speech or language disorders;

(iv) Provisions of speech and language services for the habilitation or prevention of communicative disorders; and

(v) Counseling and guidance of parents, children, and teachers regarding speech and language disorders.

(13) "Transportation" includes:

(i) Travel to and from school and between schools;

(ii) Travel in and around school buildings; and

(iii) Specialized equipment (such as special or adapted buses, lifts, and ramps), if required to provide special transportation for a handicapped child.

§ 121a.302   Residential placement.

If placement in a public or private residential program is necessary to provide special education and related services to a handicapped child, the program, including non-medical care and room and board, must be at no cost to the parents of the child.

INDIVIDUALIZED EDUCATION PROGRAMS

§ 121a.340   Definition.

As used in this part, the term "individualized education program" means a written statement for a handicapped child that is developed and implemented in accordance with § § 121a.341–121a.349.

§ 121a.341   State educational agency responsibility.

(a) *Public agencies.* The State educational agency shall insure that each public agency develops and implements an individualized education program for each of its handicapped children.

(b) *Private schools and facilities.* The State educational agency shall insure that an individualized education program is developed and implemented for each handicapped child who:

(1) Is placed in or referred to a private school or facility by a public agency; or

(2) Is enrolled in a parochial or other private school and receives special education or related services from a public agency.

Comment. This section applies to all public agencies, including other State agencies (e.g., departments of mental health and welfare), which provide special education to a handicapped child either directly, by contract or through other arrangements. Thus, if a State welfare agency contracts with a private school or facility to provide special education to a handicapped child, that agency would be responsible for insuring that an individualized education program is developed for the child.

§ 121a.342 When individualized education programs must be in effect.

(a) On October 1, 1977, and at the beginning of each school year thereafter, each public agency shall have in effect an individualized education program for every handicapped child who is receiving special education from that agency.

(b) An individualized education program must:

(1) Be in effect before special education and related services are provided to a child; and

(2) Be implemented as soon as possible following the meetings under § 121a.343.

Comment. Under paragraph (b) (2), it is expected that a handicapped child's individualized education program (IEP) will be implemented immediately following the meetings under § 121a.343. An exception to this would be (1) when the meetings occur during the summer or a vacation period, or (2) where there are circumstances which require a short delay (e.g., working out transportation arrangements). However, there can be no undue delay in providing special education and related services to the child.

§ 121a.343 Meetings.

(a) *General.* Each public agency is responsible for initiating and conducting meetings for the purpose of developing, reviewing, and revising a handicapped child's individualized education program.

(b) *Handicapped children currently served.* If the public agency has determined that a handicapped child will receive special education during school year 1977-1978, a meeting must be held early enough to insure that an individualized education program is developed by October 1, 1977.

(c) *Other handicapped children.* For a handicapped child who is not included under paragraph (b) of this action, a meeting must be held within thirty calendar days of a determination that the child needs special education and related services.

(d) *Review.* Each public agency shall initiate and conduct meetings to periodically review each child's individualized education program and if appropriate revise its provisions. A meeting must be held for this purpose at least once a year.

Comment. The dates on which agencies must have individualized education programs (IEPs) in effect are specified in § 121a.342 (October 1, 1977, and the beginning of each school year thereafter). However, except for new handicapped children (i.e., those evaluated and determined to need special education after October 1, 1977), the timing of meetings to develop, review, and revise IEPs is left to the discretion of each agency.

In order to have IEPs in effect by the dates in § 121a.342, agencies could hold meetings at the end of the school year or during the summer preceding those dates. In meeting the October 1, 1977 timeline, meetings could be conducted up through the October 1 date. Thereafter, meetings may be held any time throughout the year, as long as IEPs are in effect at the beginning of each school year.

The statute requires agencies to hold a meeting at least once each year in order to review, and if appropriate revise, each child's IEP. The timing of those meetings could be on the anniversary date of the last IEP meeting on the child, but this is left to the discretion of the agency.

§ 121a.344 Participants in meetings.

(a) *General.* The public agency shall insure that each meeting includes the following participants:

(1) A representative of the public agency, other than the child's teacher, who is qualified to provide, or supervise the provision of, special education.

(2) The child's teacher.

(3) One or both of the child's parents, subject to § 121a.-345.

(4) The child, where appropriate.

(5) Other individuals at the discretion of the parent or agency.

(b) *Evaluation personnel.* For a handicapped child who

has been evaluated for the first time, the public agency shall insure:

(1) That a member of the evaluation team participates in the meeting; or

(2) That the representative of the public agency, the child's teacher, or some other person is present at the meeting who is knowledgeable about the evaluation procedures used with the child and is familiar with the results of the evaluation.

Comment. 1. In deciding which teacher will participate in meetings on a child's individualized education program, the agency may wish to consider the following possibilities:

(a) For a handicapped child who is receiving special education, the "teacher" could be the child's special education teacher. If the child's handicap is a speech impairment, the "teacher" could be the speech-language pathologist.

(b) For a handicapped child who is being considered for placement in special education, the "teacher" could be the child's regular teacher, or a teacher qualified to provide education in the type of program in which the child may be placed, or both.

(c) If the child is not in school or has more than one teacher, the agency may designate which teacher will participate in the meeting.

2. Either the teacher or the agency representative should be qualified in the area of the child's suspected disability.

3. For a child whose primary handicap is a speech impairment, the evaluation personnel participating under paragraph (b) (1) of this section would normally be the speech-language pathologist.

§ 121a.345   Parent participation.

(a) Each public agency shall take steps to insure that one or both of the parents of the handicapped child are present at each meeting or are afforded the opportunity to participate, including:

(1) Notifying parents of the meeting early enough to insure that they will have an opportunity to attend; and

(2) Scheduling the meeting at a mutually agreed on time and place.

(b) The notice under paragraph (a) (1) of this section must indicate the purpose, time, and location of the meeting, and who will be in attendance.

(c) If neither parent can attend, the public agency shall use other methods to insure parent participation, including individual or conference telephone calls.

(d) A meeting may be conducted without a parent in attendance if the public agency is unable to convince the parents that they should attend. In this case the public agency must have a record of its attempts to arrange a mutually agreed on time and place such as:

(1) Detailed records of telephone calls made or attempted and the results of those calls.

(2) Copies of correspondence sent to the parents and any responses received, and

(3) Detailed records of visits made to the parent's home or place of employment and the results of those visits.

(e) The public agency shall take whatever action is necessary to insure that the parent understands the proceedings at a meeting, including arranging for an interpreter for parents who are deaf or whose native language is other than English.

(f) The public agency shall give the parent, on request, a copy of the individualized education program.

Comment. The notice in paragraph (a) could also inform parents that they may bring other people to the meeting. As indicated in paragraph (c), the procedure used to notify parents (whether oral or written or both) is left to the discretion of the agency, but the agency must keep a record of its efforts to contact parents.

§ 121a.346 Content of individualized education program.

The individualized education program for each child must include:

(a) A statement of the child's present levels of educational performance;

(b) A statement of annual goals, including short term instructional objectives;

(c) A statement of the specific special education and related services to be provided to the child, and the extent to which the child will be able to participate in regular educational programs;

(d) The projected dates for initiation of services and the anticipated duration of the services; and

(e) Appropriate objective criteria and evaluation procedures and schedules for determining, on at least an annual basis, whether the short term instructional objectives are being achieved.

§ 121a.347   Private school placements.

(a) *Developing individualized education programs.* (1) Before a public agency places a handicapped child in, or refers a child to, a private school or facility, the agency shall initiate and conduct a meeting to develop an individualized education program for the child in accordance with § 121a.343.

(2) The agency shall insure that a representative of the private school facility attends the meeting. If the representative cannot attend, the agency shall use other methods to insure participation by the private school or facility, including individual or conference telephone calls.

(3) The public agency shall also develop an individualized educational program for each handicapped child who was placed in a private school or facility by the agency before the effective date of these regulations.

(b) *Reviewing and revising individualized education programs.* (1) After a handicapped child enters a private school or facility, any meetings to review and revise the child's individualized education program may be initiated and conducted by the private school or facility at the discretion of the public agency.

(2) If the private school or facility initiates and conducts these meetings, the public agency shall insure that the parents and an agency representative:

(i) Are involved in any decision about the child's individualized education program; and

(ii) Agree to any proposed changes in the program before those changes are implemented.

(c) *Responsibility.* Even if a private school or facility implements a child's individualized education program, responsibility for compliance with this part remains with the public agency and the State educational agency.

§ 121a.348 Handicapped children in parochial or other private schools.

If a handicapped child is enrolled in a parochial or other private school and receives special education or related services from a public agency, the public agency shall:

(a) Initiate and conduct meetings to develop, review, and revise an individualized education program for the child, in accordance with § 121a.343; and

(b) Insure that a representative of the parochial or other private school attends each meeting. If the representative cannot attend, the agency shall use other methods to insure participation by the private school, including individual or conference telephone calls.

§ 121a.349 Individualized education program—accountability.

Each public agency must provide special education and related services to a handicapped child in accordance with an individualized education program. However, Part B of the Act does not require that any agency, teacher, or other person be held accountable if a child does not achieve the growth projected in the annual goals and objectives.

Comment. This section is intended to relieve concerns that the individualized education program constitutes a guarantee by the public agency and the teacher that a child will progress at a specified rate. However, this section does not relieve agencies and teachers from making good faith efforts to assist the child in achieving the objectives and goals listed in the individualized education program. Further, the section does not limit a parent's right to complain and ask for revisions of the child's program, or to invoke due process procedures, if the parent feels that these efforts are not being made.

COMPREHENSIVE SYSTEM
OF PERSONNEL DEVELOPMENT

§ 121a.380   Scope of system.

Each annual program plan must include a description of programs and procedures for the development and implementation of a comprehensive system of personnel development which includes:

(a) The inservice training of general and special educational instructional, related services, and support personnel;

(b) Procedures to insure that all personnel necessary to carry out the purposes of the Act are qualified (as defined in § 121a.12 of Subpart A) and that activities sufficient to carry out this personnel development plan are scheduled; and

(c) Effective procedures for acquiring and disseminating to teachers and administrators of programs for handicapped children significant information derived from educational research, demonstration, and similar projects, and for adopting, where appropriate, promising educational practices and materials developed through those projects.

§ 121a.381   Participation of other agencies and institutions.

(a) The State educational agency must insure that all public and private institutions of higher education, and other agencies and organizations (including representatives of handicapped, parent, and other advocacy organizations) in the State which have an interest in the preparation of personnel for the education of handicapped children, have an opportunity to participate fully in the development, review, and annual updating of the comprehensive system of personnel development.

(b) The annual program plan must describe the nature and extent of participation under paragraph (a) of this section and must describe responsibilities of the State educational agency, local educational agencies, public and private institutions of higher education, and other agencies:

(1) With respect to the comprehensive system as a whole, and

(2) With respect to the personnel development plan under § 121a.383.

§ 121a.382 Inservice training.

(a) As used in this section, "inservice training" means any training other than that received by an individual in a full-time program which leads to a degree.

(b) Each annual program plan must provide that the State educational agency:

(1) Conducts an annual needs assessment to determine if a sufficient number of qualified personnel are available in the State; and

(2) Initiates inservice personnel development programs based on the assessed needs of Statewide significance related to the implementation of the Act.

(c) Each annual program plan must include the results of the needs assessment under paragraph (b) (1) of this section, broken out by need for new personnel and need for retrained personnel.

(d) The State educational agency may enter into contracts with institutions of higher education, local educational agencies or other agencies, institutions, or organizations (which may include parent, handicapped, or other advocacy organizations), to carry out:

(1) Experimental or innovative personnel development programs;

(2) Development or modification of instructional materials; and

(3) Dissemination of significant information derived from educational research and demonstration projects.

(e) Each annual program plan must provide that the State educational agency insures that ongoing inservice training programs are available to all personnel who are engaged in the education of handicapped children, and that these programs include:

(1) The use of incentives which insure participation by teachers (such as released time, payment for participation, options for academic credit, salary step credit, certification renewal, or updating professional skills);

(2) The involvement of local staff; and

(3) The use of innovative practices which have been found to be effective.

(f) Each annual program plan must:

(1) Describe the process used in determining the inservice training needs of personnel engaged in the education of handicapped children;

(2) Identify the areas in which training is needed (such as individualized education programs, non-discriminatory testing, least restrictive environment, procedural safeguards, and surrogate parents);

(3) Specify the groups requiring training (such as special teachers, regular teachers, administrators, psychologists, speech-language pathologists, audiologists, physical education teachers, therapeutic recreation specialists, physical therapists, occupational therapists, medical personnel, parents, volunteers, hearing officers, and surrogate parents);

(4) Describe the content and nature of training for each area under paragraph (f) (2) of this section;

(5) Describe how the training will be provided in terms of (i) geographical scope (such as Statewide, regional, or local), and (ii) staff training source (such as college and university staffs, State and local educational agency personnel, and non-agency personnel);

(6) Specify: (i) The funding sources to be used, and

(ii) The time frame for providing it; and

(7) Specify procedures for effective evaluation of the extent to which program objectives are met.

§ 121a.383 Personnel development plan.

Each annual program plan must: (a) Include a personnel

development plan which provides a structure for personnel planning and focuses on preservice and inservice education needs;

(b) Describe the results of the needs assessment under § 121a.382 (b) (1) with respect to identifying needed areas of training, and assigning priorities to those areas; and

(c) Identify the target populations for personnel development, including general education and special education instructional and administrative personnel, support personnel, and other personnel (such as paraprofessionals, parents, surrogate parents, and volunteers).

§ 121a.384 Dissemination.

(a) Each annual program plan must include a description of the State's procedures for acquiring, reviewing, and disseminating to general and special educational instructional and support personnel, administrators of programs for handicapped children, and other interested agencies and organizations (including parent, handicapped, and other advocacy organizations) significant information and promising practices derived from educational research, demonstration, and other projects.

(b) Dissemination includes:

(1) Making those personnel, administrators, agencies, and organizations aware of the information and practices;

(2) Training designed to enable the establishment of innovative programs and practices targeted on identified local needs; and

(3) Use of instructional materials and other media for personnel development and instructional programming.

§ 121a.385 Adoption of educational practices.

(a) Each annual program plan must provide for a statewide system designed to adopt, where appropriate, promising educational practices and materials proven effective through research and demonstration.

(b) Each annual program plan must provide for thorough reassessment of educational practices used in the State.

(c) Each annual program plan must provide for the identification of State, local, and regional resources (human and material) which will assist in meeting the State's personnel preparation needs.

§ 121a.386   Evaluation.

Each annual program plan must include:

(a) Procedures for evaluating the overall effectiveness of:

(1) The comprehensive system of personnel development in meeting the needs for personnel, and

(2) The procedures for administration of the system; and

(b) A description of the monitoring activities that will be undertaken to assure the implementation of the comprehensive system of personnel development.

§ 121a.403   Placement of children by parents.

(a) If a handicapped child has available a free appropriate public education and the parents choose to place the child in a private school or facility, the public agency is not required by this part to pay for the child's education at the private school or facility. However, the public agency shall make services available to the child as provided under § § 121a.450–121a.460.

(b) Disagreements between a parent and a public agency regarding the availability of a program appropriate for the child, and the question of financial responsibility, are subject to the due process procedures under § § 121a.500–121a.514 of Subpart E.

§ 121a.503   Independent educational evaluation.

(a) *General.* (1) The parents of a handicapped child have the right under this part to obtain an independent educational evaluation of the child, subject to paragraphs (b) through (e) of this section.

(2) Each public agency shall provide to parents, on request, information about where an independent educational evaluation may be obtained.

(3) For the purposes of this part:

(i) "Independent educational evaluation" means an

evaluation conducted by a qualified examiner who is not employed by the public agency responsible for the education of the child in question.

(ii) "Public expense" means that the public agency either pays for the full cost of the evaluation or insures that the evaluation is otherwise provided at no cost to the parent, consistent with § 121a.301 of Subpart C.

(b) *Parent right to evaluation at public expense.* A parent has the right to an independent educational evaluation at public expense if the parent disagrees with an evaluation obtained by the public agency. However, the public agency may initiate a hearing under § 121a.506 of this subpart to show that its evaluation is appropriate. If the final decision is that the evaluation is appropriate, the parent still has the right to an independent educational evaluation, but not at public expense.

(c) *Parent initiated evaluations.* If the parent obtains an independent educational evaluation at private expense, the results of the evaluation:

(1) Must be considered by the public agency in any decision made with respect to the provision of a free appropriate public education to the child, and

(2) May be presented as evidence at a hearing under this subpart regarding that child.

(d) *Requests for evaluations by hearing officers.* If a hearing officer requests an independent educational evaluation as part of a hearing, the cost of the evaluation must be at public expense.

(e) *Agency criteria.* Whenever an independent evaluation is at public expense, the criteria under which the evaluation is obtained, including the location of the evaluation and the qualifications of the examiner, must be the same as the criteria which the public agency uses when it initiates an evaluation.

§ 121a.504   Prior notice; parent consent.

(a) *Notice.* Written notice which meets the requirements under § 121a.505 must be given to the parents of a handicapped child a reasonable time before the public agency:

(1) Proposes to initiate or change the identification,

evaluation, or educational placement of the child or the provision of a free appropriate public education to the child, or

(2) Refuses to initiate or change the identification, evaluation, or educational placement of the child or the provision of a free appropriate public education to the child.

(b) *Consent.* (1) Parental consent must be obtained before:

(i) Conducting a preplacement evaluation; and

(ii) Initial placement of a handicapped child in a program providing special education and related services.

(2) Except for preplacement evaluation and initial placement, consent may not be required as a condition of any benefit to the parent or child.

(c) *Procedures where parent refuses consent.* (1) Where State law requires parental consent before a handicapped child is evaluated or initially provided special education and related services, State procedures govern the public agency in overriding a parent's refusal to consent.

(2) (i) Where there is no State law requiring consent before a handicapped child is evaluated or initially provided special education and related services, the public agency may use the hearing procedures in § § 121a.506—121a.508 to determine if the child may be evaluated or initially provided special education and related services without parental consent.

(ii) If the hearing officer upholds the agency, the agency may evaluate or initially provide special education and related services to the child without the parent's consent, subject to the parent's rights under § § 121a.510—121a.513.

Comment. 1. Any changes in a child's special education program, after the initial placement, are not subject to parental consent under Part B, but are subject to the prior notice requirement in paragraph (a) and the individualized education program requirements in Subpart C.

2. Paragraph (c) means that where State law requires parental consent before evaluation or before special education and related services are initially provided, and the parent refuses (or otherwise withholds) consent, State procedures, such as obtaining a court order authorizing the public agency to conduct

the evaluation or provide the education and related services, must be followed.

If, however, there is no legal requirement for consent outside of these regulations, the public agency may use the due process procedures under this subpart to obtain a decision to allow the evaluation or services without parental consent. The agency must notify the parent of its actions, and the parent has appeal rights as well as rights at the hearing itself.

§ 121a.505 Content of notice.

(a) The notice under § 121a.504 must include:

(1) A full explanation of all of the procedural safeguards available to the parents under Subpart E;

(2) A description of the action proposed or refused by the agency, an explanation of why the agency proposes or refuses to take the action, and a description of any options the agency considered and the reasons why those options were rejected;

(3) A description of each evaluation procedure, test, record, or report the agency uses as a basis for the proposal or refusal; and

(4) A description of any other factors which are relevant to the agency's proposal or refusal.

(b) The notice must be:

(1) Written in language understandable to the general public, and

(2) Provided in the native language of the parent or other mode of communication used by the parent, unless it is clearly not feasible to do so.

(c) If the native language or other mode of communication of the parent is not a written language, the State or local educational agency shall take steps to insure:

(1) That the notice is translated orally or by other means to the parent in his or her native language or other mode of communication;

(2) That the parent understands the content of the notice; and

(3) That there is written evidence that the requirements in paragraph (c) (1) and (2) of this section have been met.

§ 121a.506   Impartial due process hearing.

(a) A parent or a public educational agency may initiate a hearing on any of the matters described in § 121a.504 (a) (1) and (2).

(b) The hearing must be conducted by the State educational agency or the public agency directly responsible for the education of the child, as determined under State statute, State regulation, or a written policy of the State educational agency.

(c) The public agency shall inform the parent of any free or low-cost legal and other relevant services available in the area if:

(1) The parent requests the information; or

(2) The parent or the agency initiates a hearing under this section.

Comment. Many States have pointed to the success of using mediation as an intervening step prior to conducting a formal due process hearing. Although the process of mediation is not required by the statute or these regulations, an agency may wish to suggest mediation in disputes concerning the identification, evaluation, and educational placement of handicapped children, and the provision of a free appropriate public education to those children. Mediations have been conducted by members of State educational agencies or local educational agency personnel who were not previously involved in the particular case. In many cases, mediation leads to resolution of differences between parents and agencies without the development of an adversarial relationship and with minimal emotional stress. However, mediation may not be used to deny or delay a parent's rights under this subpart.

§ 121a.507   Impartial hearing officer.

(a) A hearing may not be conducted:

(1) By a person who is an employee of a public agency which is involved in the education or care of the child, or

(2) By any person having a personal or professional interest which would conflict with his or her objectivity in the hearing.

(b) A person who otherwise qualifies to conduct a hearing under paragraph (a) of this section is not an employee of the agency solely because he or she is paid by the agency to serve as a hearing officer.

(c) Each public agency shall keep a list of the persons who serve as hearing officers. The list must include a statement of the qualifications of each of those persons.

§ 121a.508   Hearing rights.

(a) Any party to a hearing has the right to:

(1) Be accompanied and advised by counsel and by individuals with special knowledge or training with respect to the problems of handicapped children;

(2) Present evidence and confront, cross-examine, and compel the attendance of witnesses;

(3) Prohibit the introduction of any evidence at the hearing that has not been disclosed to that party at least five days before the hearing;

(4) Obtain a written or electronic verbatim record of the hearing;

(5) Obtain written findings of fact and decisions. (The public agency shall transmit those findings and decisions, after deleting any personally identifiable information, to the State advisory panel established under Subpart F).

(b) Parents involved in hearings must be given the right to:

(1) Have the child who is the subject of the hearing present; and

(2) Open the hearing to the public.

§ 121a.509   Hearing decision; appeal.

A decision made in a hearing conducted under this subpart is final, unless a party to the hearing appeals the decision under § 121a.510 or § 121a.511.

§ 121a.510   Administrative appeal; impartial review.

(a) If the hearing is conducted by a public agency other than the State educational agency, any party aggrieved by the findings and decision in the hearing may appeal to the State educational agency.

(b) If there is an appeal, the State educational agency shall conduct an impartial review of the hearing. The official conducting the review shall:

(1) Examine the entire hearing record;

(2) Insure that the procedures at the hearing were consistent with the requirements of due process;

(3) Seek additional evidence if necessary. If a hearing is held to receive additional evidence, the rights in § 121a.508 apply;

(4) Afford the parties an opportunity for oral or written argument, or both, at the discretion of the reviewing official;

(5) Make an independent decision on completion of the review; and

(6) Give a copy of written findings and the decision to the parties.

(c) The decision made by the reviewing official is final, unless a party brings a civil action under § 121a.512.

Comment. 1. The State educational agency may conduct its review either directly or through another State agency acting on its behalf. However, the State educational agency remains responsible for the final decision on review.

2. All parties have the right to continue to be represented by counsel at the State administrative review level, whether or not the reviewing official determines that a further hearing is necessary. If the reviewing official decides to hold a hearing to receive additional evidence, the other rights in section 121a.508, relating to hearings, also apply.

§ 121a.511   Civil action.

Any party aggrieved by the findings and decision made in a hearing who does not have the right to appeal under § 121a.510 of this subpart, and any party aggrieved by the decision of a reviewing officer under § 121a.510 has the right to bring a civil action under section 615 (e) (2) of the Act.

§ 121a.512 Timeliness and convenience of hearings and reviews.

(a) The public agency shall insure that not later than 45 days after the receipt of a request for a hearing:

(1) A final decision is reached in the hearing; and

(2) A copy of the decision is mailed to each of the parties.

(b) The State educational agency shall insure that not later than 30 days after the receipt of a request for a review:

(1) A final decision is reached in the review; and

(2) A copy of the decision is mailed to each of the parties.

(c) A hearing or reviewing officer may grant specific extensions of time beyond the periods set out in paragraphs (a) and (b) of this section at the request of either party.

(d) Each hearing and each review involving oral arguments must be conducted at a time and place which is reasonably convenient to the parents and child involved.

§ 121a.513 Child's status during proceedings.

(a) During the pendency of any administrative or judicial proceeding regarding a complaint, unless the public agency and the parents of the child agree otherwise, the child involved in the complaint must remain in his or her present educational placement.

(b) If the complaint involves an application for initial admission to public school, the child, with the consent of the parents, must be placed in the public school program until the completion of all the proceedings.

Comment. Section 121a.513 does not permit a child's placement to be changed during a complaint proceeding, unless the parents and agency agree otherwise. While the placement may not be changed, this does not preclude the agency from using its normal procedures for dealing with children who are endangering themselves or others.

§ 121a.514 Surrogate parents.

(a) *General.* Each public agency shall insure that the

rights of a child are protected when:

(1) No parent (as defined in § 121a.10) can be identified;

(2) The public agency, after reasonable efforts, cannot discover the whereabouts of a parent; or

(3) The child is a ward of the State under the laws of that State.

(b) *Duty of public agency.* The duty of a public agency under paragraph (a) of this section includes the assignment of an individual to act as a surrogate for the parents. This must include a method (1) for determining whether a child needs a surrogate parent, and (2) for assigning a surrogate parent to the child.

(c) *Criteria for selection of surrogates.* (1) The public agency may select a surrogate parent in any way permitted under State law.

(2) Public agencies shall insure that a person selected as a surrogate:

(i) Has no interest that conflicts with the interests of the child he or she represents; and

(ii) Has knowledge and skills that insure adequate representation of the child.

(d) *Non-employee requirement; compensation.* (1) A person assigned as a surrogate may not be an employee of a public agency which is involved in the education or care of the child.

(2) A person who otherwise qualifies to be a surrogate parent under paragraph (c) and (d) (1) of this section, is not an employee of the agency solely because he or she is paid by the agency to serve as a surrogate parent.

(e) *Responsibilities.* The surrogate parent may represent the child in all matters relating to:

(1) The identification, evaluation, and educational placement of the child, and

(2) The provision of a free appropriate public education to the child.

PROTECTION IN EVALUATION PROCEDURES

§ 121a.530 General.

(a) Each State educational agency shall insure that each

public agency establishes and implements procedures which meet the requirements of § § 121a.530—121a.534.

(b) Testing and evaluation materials and procedures used for the purposes of evaluation and placement of handicapped children must be selected and administered so as not to be racially or culturally discriminatory.

§ 121a.531 Preplacement evaluation.

Before any action is taken with respect to the initial placement of a handicapped child in a special education program, a full and individual evaluation of the child's educational needs must be conducted in accordance with the requirements of § 121a.532.

§ 121a.532 Evaluation procedures.

State and local educational agencies shall insure, at a minimum, that:

(a) Tests and other evaluation materials:

(1) Are provided and administered in the child's native language or other mode of communication, unless it is clearly not feasible to do so;

(2) Have been validated for the specific purpose for which they are used; and

(3) Are administered by trained personnel in conformance with the instructions provided by their producer;

(b) Tests and other evaluation materials include those tailored to assess specific areas of educational need and not merely those which are designed to provide a single general intelligence quotient;

(c) Tests are selected and administered so as best to ensure that when a test is administered to a child with impaired sensory, manual, or speaking skills, the test results accurately reflect the child's aptitude or achievement level or whatever other factors the test purports to measure, rather than reflecting the child's impaired sensory, manual, or speaking skills (except where those skills are the factors which the test purports to measure);

(d) No single procedure is used as the sole criterion for

determining an appropriate educational program for a child; and

(e) The evaluation is made by a multidisciplinary team or group of persons, including at least one teacher or other specialist with knowledge in the area of suspected disability.

(f) The child is assessed in all areas related to the suspected disability, including, where appropriate, health, vision, hearing, social and emotional status, general intelligence, academic performance, communicative status, and motor abilities.

Comment. Children who have a speech impairment as their primary handicap may not need a complete battery of assessments (e.g., psychological, physical, or adaptive behavior). However, a qualified speech-language pathologist would (1) evaluate each speech impaired child using procedures that are appropriate for the diagnosis and appraisal of speech and language disorders, and (2) where necessary, make referrals for additional assessments needed to make an appropriate placement decision.

§ 121a.533 Placement procedures.

(a) In interpreting evaluation data and in making placement decisions, each public agency shall:

(1) Draw upon information from a variety of sources, including aptitude and achievement tests, teacher recommendations, physical condition, social or cultural background, and adaptive behavior;

(2) Insure that information obtained from all of these sources is documented and carefully considered;

(3) Insure that the placement decision is made by a group of persons, including persons knowledgeable about the child, the meaning of the evaluation data, and the placement options; and

(4) Insure that the placement decision is made in conformity with the least restrictive environment rules in § § 121a.550–121a.554.

(b) If a determination is made that a child is handicapped and needs special education and related services, an individualized education program must be developed for the child in accordance with § § 121a.340–121a.349 of Subpart C.

Comment. Paragraph (a) (1) includes a list of examples of sources that may be used by a public agency in making placement decisions. The agency would not have to use all the sources in every instance. The point of the requirement is to insure that more than one source is used in interpreting evaluation data and in making placement decisions. For example, while all of the named sources would have to be used for a child whose suspected disability is mental retardation, they would not be necessary for certain other handicapped children, such as a child who has a severe articulation disorder as his primary handicap. For such a child, the speech-language pathologist, in complying with the multisource requirement, might use (1) a standardized test of articulation, and (2) observation of the child's articulation behavior in conversational speech.

§ 121a.534 Reevaluation.

Each State and local educational agency shall insure:

(a) That each handicapped child's individualized education program is reviewed in accordance with § § 121a.340–121a.349 of Subpart C, and

(b) That an evaluation of the child, based on procedures which meet the requirements under § 121a.532, is conducted every three years or more frequently if conditions warrant or if the child's parent or teacher requests an evaluation.

LEAST RESTRICTIVE ENVIRONMENT

§ 121a.550 General.

(a) Each State educational agency shall insure that each public agency establishes and implements procedures which meet the requirements of § § 121a.550–121a.556.

(b) Each public agency shall insure:

(1) That to the maximum extent appropriate, handicapped children, including children in public or private institutions or other care facilities, are educated with children who are not handicapped, and

(2) That special classes, separate schooling or other removal of handicapped children from the regular educational environment occurs only when the nature or severity of the handicap is such that education in regular classes with the use of supplementary aids and services cannot be achieved satisfactorily.

§ 121a.551   Continuum of alternative placements.

(a) Each public agency shall insure that a continuum of alternative placements is available to meet the needs of handicapped children for special education and related services.

(b) The continuum required under paragraph (a) of this section must:

(1) Include the alternative placements listed in the definition of special education under § 121a.13 of Subpart A (instruction in regular classes, special classes, special schools, home instruction, and instruction in hospitals and institutions), and

(2) Make provision for supplementary services (such as resource room or itinerant instruction) to be provided in conjunction with regular class placement.

§ 121a.552   Placements.

Each public agency shall insure that:

(a) Each handicapped child's educational placement:

(1) Is determined at least annually,

(2) Is based on his or her individualized education program, and

(3) Is as close as possible to the child's home;

(b) The various alternative placements included under § 121a.551 are available to the extent necessary to implement the individualized education program for each handicapped child;

(c) Unless a handicapped child's individualized education program requires some other arrangement, the child is educated in the school which he or she would attend if not handicapped; and

(d) In selecting the least restrictive environment, consideration is given to any potential harmful effect on the child or on the quality of services which he or she needs.

§ 121a.554   Children in public or private institutions.

Each State educational agency shall make arrangements with public and private institutions (such as a memorandum of agreement or special implementation procedures) as may be necessary to insure that § 121a.550 is effectively implemented.

CONFIDENTIALITY OF INFORMATION

§ 121a.560   Definitions.

As used in this subpart:

"Destruction" means physical destruction or removal of personal identifiers from information so that the information is no longer personally identifiable.

"Education records" means the type of records covered under the definition of "education records" in Part 99 of this title (the regulations implementing the Family Educational Rights and Privacy Act of 1974).

"Participating agency" means any agency or institution which collects, maintains, or uses personally identifiable information, or from which information is obtained, under this part.

§ 121a.561   Notice to parents.

(a) The State educational agency shall give notice which is adequate to fully inform parents about the requirements under § 121a.128 of Subpart B, including:

(1) A description of the extent to which the notice is given in the native languages of the various population groups in the State;

(2) A description of the children on whom personally identifiable information is maintained, the types of information sought, the methods the State intends to use in gathering the information (including the sources from whom information is gathered), and the uses to be made of the information;

(3) A summary of the policies and procedures which par-

ticipating agencies must follow regarding storage, disclosure to third parties, retention, and destruction of personally identifiable information; and

(4) A description of all of the rights of parents and children regarding this information, including the rights under section 438 of the General Education Provisions Act and Part 99 of this title (the Family Educational Rights and Privacy Act of 1974, and implementing regulations).

(b) Before any major identification, location, or evaluation activity, the notice must be published or announced in newspapers or other media, or both, with circulation adequate to notify parents throughout the State of the activity.

§ 121a.562   Access rights.

(a) Each participating agency shall permit parents to inspect and review any education records relating to their children which are collected, maintained, or used by the agency under this part. The agency shall comply with a request without unnecessary delay and before any meeting regarding an individualized education program or hearing relating to the identification, evaluation, or placement of the child, and in no case more than 45 days after the request has been made.

(b) The right to inspect and review education records under this section includes:

(1) The right to a response from the participating agency to reasonable requests for explanations and interpretations of the records;

(2) The right to request that the agency provide copies of the records containing the information if failure to provide those copies would effectively prevent the parent from exercising the right to inspect and review the records; and

(3) The right to have a representative of the parent inspect and review the records.

(c) An agency may presume that the parent has authority to inspect and review records relating to his or her child unless the agency has been advised that the parent does not have the authority under applicable State law governing such matters as guardianship, separation, and divorce.

§ 121a.563   Record of access.

Each participating agency shall keep a record of parties obtaining access to education records collected, maintained, or used under this part (except access by parents and authorized employees of the participating agency), including the name of the party, the date access was given, and the purpose for which the party is authorized to use the records.

§ 121a.565   List of types and locations of information.

Each participating agency shall provide parents on request a list of the types and locations of education records collected, maintained, or used by the agency.

§ 121a.566   Fees.

(a) A participating education agency may charge a fee for copies of records which are made for parents under this part if the fee does not effectively prevent the parents from exercising their right to inspect and review those records.

(b) A participating agency may not charge a fee to search for or to retrieve information under this part.

§ 121a.567   Amendment of records at parent's request.

(a) A parent who believes that information in education records collected, maintained, or used under this part is inaccurate or misleading or violates the privacy or other rights of the child, may request the participating agency which maintains the information to amend the information.

(b) The agency shall decide whether to amend the information in accordance with the request within a reasonable period of time of receipt of the request.

(c) If the agency decides to refuse to amend the information in accordance with the request, it shall inform the parent of the refusal, and advise the parent of the right to a hearing under § 121a.568.

§ 121a.568   Opportunity for a hearing.

The agency shall, on request, provide an opportunity for a hearing to challenge information in education records to insure that it is not inaccurate, misleading, or otherwise in violation of the privacy or other rights of the child.

§ 121a.569   Result of hearing.

(a) If, as a result of the hearing, the agency decides that the information is inaccurate, misleading, or otherwise in violation of the privacy or other rights of the child, it shall amend the information accordingly and so inform the parent in writing.

(b) If, as a result of the hearing, the agency decides that the information is not inaccurate, misleading, or otherwise in violation of the privacy or other rights of the child, it shall inform the parent of the right to place in the records it maintains on the child a statement commenting on the information or setting forth any reasons for disagreeing with the decision of the agency.

(c) Any explanation placed in the records of the child under this section must:

(1) Be maintained by the agency as part of the records of the child as long as the record or contested portion is maintained by the agency; and

(2) If the records of the child or the contested portion is disclosed by the agency to any party, the explanation must also be disclosed to the party.

§ 121a.570   Hearing procedures.

A hearing held under § 121a.568 of this subpart must be conducted according to the procedures under § 99.22 of this title.

§ 121a.571   Consent.

(a) Parental consent must be obtained before personally identifiable information is:

(1) Disclosed to anyone other than officials of participating agencies collecting or using the information under this part, subject to paragraph (b) of this section; or

(2) Used for any purpose other than meeting a requirement under this part.

(b) An educational agency or institution subject to Part 99 of this title may not release information from education records to participating agencies without parental consent unless authorized to do so under Part 99 of this title.

(c) The State educational agency shall include policies and procedures in its annual program plan which are used in the event that a parent refuses to provide consent under this section.

§ 121a.572   Safeguards.

(a) Each participating agency shall protect the confidentiality of personally identifiable information at collection, storage, disclosure, and destruction stages.

(b) One official at each participating agency shall assume responsibility for insuring the confidentiality of any personally identifiable information.

(c) All persons collecting or using personally identifiable information must receive training or instruction regarding the State's policies and procedures under § 121a.129 of Subpart B and Part 99 of this title.

(d) Each participating agency shall maintain, for public inspection, a current listing of the names and positions of those employees within the agency who may have access to personally identifiable information.

§ 121a.573   Destruction of information.

(a) The public agency shall inform parents when personally identifiable information collected, maintained, or used under this part is no longer needed to provide educational services to the child.

(b) The information must be destroyed at the request of the parents. However, a permanent record of a student's name, address, and phone number, his or her grades, attendance record, classes attended, grade level completed, and year completed may be maintained without time limitation.

Comment. Under section 121a.573, the personally identifiable information on a handicapped child may be retained permanently unless the parents request that it be destroyed. Destruction of records is the best protection against improper and unauthorized disclosure. However, the records may be needed for other purposes. In informing parents about their rights under this section, the agency should remind them that the records may be needed by the child or the parents for social security benefits or other purposes. If the parents request that the information be destroyed, the agency may retain the information in paragraph (b).

Resources

Publications

Amicus (newsletter), National Center for Law and the Handicapped, 1235 North Eddy St., South Bend, Ind. 46617.

Barriers and Bridges (book), California Advisory Council on Vocational Education, 708 Tenth St., Sacramento, Cal. 95184 (1977).

Children, Parents and School Records (book), Rioux, J., and Sandow, S., National Committee for Citizens in Education, Wilde Lake Village Green, Columbia, M.D. 21044 (1974).

Closer Look (newsletter), National Information Center for the Handicapped, Box 1492, Wash., D.C. 20013.

Education of the Handicapped (newsletter), Capitol Publications, Suite G-12, 2430 Pennsylvania Ave., N.W., Wash., D.C. 20037.

Law and Behavior (newsletter), Research Press, 2612 N. Mattis, Champaign, Ill. 61820.

Legal Rights of the Mentally Handicapped (book, 3 vols.), Ennis, B., and Friedman, P., Practicing Law Institute, 1133 Avenue of the Americas, New York, N.Y. 10036 (1974).

Mental Disability Law Reporter (newsletter), American Bar Association Commission of the Mentally Disabled, 1800 M St., N.W., Wash., D.C. 20036.

Mental Health Law Project Report (newsletter), Mental Health Law Project, 1220 19th St., N.W., Wash., D.C. 20036.

Mental Retardation and the Law: Status Report on Current Court Cases (newsletter), H.E.W., President's Committee on Mental Retardation, Wash., D.C. 20201.

Programs for the Handicapped (newsletter), Office for Handicapped Individuals, H.E.W., Wash., D.C. 20201.

The Rights of Handicapped Children (journal, 2 vols.), *Harvard Educational Review, 43* (4), Nov. 1973 and *44* (1), Feb. 1974.

The Rights of Mentally Retarded Persons (book), Friedman, P., American Civil Liberties Union. Published by Avon Books, 250 W. 55th St., New York, N.Y. 10019 (1976).

School Suspensions: Are They Helping Children? (book), Children's Defense Fund, 1520 New Hampshire, N.W., Wash., D.C. 20036 (1975).

Organizations

American Association for the Education of the Severely/Profoundly Handicapped, P.O. Box 15287, Seattle, Wash. 98115.

American Association on Mental Deficiency, 5201 Connecticut Ave., N.W., Wash., D.C. 20015.

American Bar Association Commission on the Mentally Disabled, 1800 M St., N.W., Wash., D.C. 20036.

American Coalition of Citizens With Disabilities, 1346 Connecticut Ave., N.W., Wash., D.C. 20036.

Association for Children with Learning Disabilities, 5225 Grace St., Pittsburgh, Penn. 15236.

Children's Defense Fund, 1520 New Hampshire, N.W., Wash., D.C. 20036.

Council on Exceptional Children, 1920 Association Drive, Reston, Va. 22091.

Mental Health Law Project, 1220 19th St., N.W., Wash., D.C. 20036.

National Association for Mental Health, 1800 North Kent, Arlington, Va. 22209.

National Association for Retarded Citizens, 2709 Avenue E, East, Arlington, Tex. 76011.

National Center for Law and the Handicapped, 1236 N. Eddy St., South Bend, Ind. 46617.

National Society for Autistic Children, 621 Central Avenue, Albany, N.Y. 12206.

References

Books and Periodicals

Coulter, W. A., & Morrow, H. W. *The concept and measurement of adaptive behavior within the scope of psychological assessment.* Austin, Tex.: Texas Regional Resource Center, 1977.

Masters, B., & Hylander, P. *Identification assessment and placement forms and procedures to assure compliance with P. L. 94-142 and P. L. 93-112, Section 504.* Edinburg, Tex.: Region One Education Service Center, 1977.

Porter, S. *The Los Angeles Herald Examiner.* October 17, 1976. As quoted in California Advisory Council on Vocational Education, *Barriers and bridges.* Sacramento: California Advisory Council on Vocational Education, 1977.

Rioux, J., & Sandow, S. *Children, parents and school records.* Columbia, Md.: National Committee for Citizens in Education, 1974.

Task Force on Children Out of School. *The way we go to school: The exclusion of children in Boston.* Boston: Beacon Press, 1971.

Weatherly, R., & Lipsky, M. Street-level bureaucrats and institutional innovations: Implementing special education reform. *Harvard Education Review, 47* (2), 171-197.

Court cases

Adams v. Califano, 430 F. Supp. 180 (D.D.C. 1977).

Bartley v. Kremens, 402 F. Supp. 1039 (E.D. Pa. 1975), 45 *U.S. Law Week* 4451 (1977).

Beattie v. State Board of Education, 172 N.W. 153 (1919).

Beauchamp v. Jones, 413 F. Supp. 646 (D. Del. 1976).

Brown v. Board of Education, 347 U.S. 483 (1954).

Cherry v. Mathews, 419 F. Supp. 922 (D.D.C. 1976).

Crowder v. Riles, No. CA-000384 (Super. Ct., Los Angeles County, Dec. 20, 1976).

Davis v. Wynne, No. CV-176-44 (S.D. Ga., Consent Decree entered May 21, 1977).

Diana v. State Board of Education, Civ. Act. No. 70-37 RFP (N.D. Cal. Jan. 7, 1970 and June 18, 1973).

Donnie R. v. Wood, No. 77-1360 (D.S.C., Consent Decree entered August 22, 1977).

Fialkowski v. Shapp, 405 F. Supp. 946 (E.D. Pa. 1975).

Frederick L. v. Thomas, 408 F. Supp. 832 (E.D. Pa. 1976).

Goldberg v. Kelley, 397 U.S. 245 (1969).

Goss v. Lopez, 419 U.S. 565 (1975).

Hairston v. Drosick, 423 F. Supp. 180 (S.D. W.Va. 1976).

Halderman v. Pennhurst, 446 F. Supp. 1295 (E.D. Pa. 1977).

In Re Downey, 340 N.Y.S. 2d 687 (Fam. Ct., New York 1973).

In Re Gault, 387 U.S. 1 (1967).

In Re K, 347 N.Y.S. 2d 271 (Fam. Ct., New York 1973).

In the Matter of Richard G., (N.Y.S.Ct., App. Div., 2nd Dept., May 17, 1976).

In the Matter of Tracy Ann Cox, No. H-4721-75 (N.Y. Fam. Ct., Queens County, April 8, 1976).

Interest of G. H., 218 N.W. 2d 441 (1974).

J. L. v. Parham, 412 F. Supp. 112 (M.D. Ga. 1976), stay denied, 412 F. Supp. 141 (M.D. Ga. 1976).

Kruse v. Campbell, 431 F. Supp. 180 (E.D. Va. 1977), vacated and remanded to be decided solely on Section 504 grounds, 98 S. Ct. 38 (1977).

Larry P. v. Riles, preliminary injunction 343 F. Supp. 1306 (N.D. Cal. 1972), aff'd 502 F. 2d 963 (9th Cir. 1974).

Lau v. Nichols, 414 U.S. 563 (1974).

Lemon v. Bossier Parish, 240 F. Supp. 790 (W.D. La. 1965), aff'd 370 F. 2d 847 (5th Cir. 1967), cert. denied, 388 U.S. 911 (1967).

Lopez v. Williams, 372 F. Supp. 1279 (S.D. Ohio 1973).

Mattie T. v. Holladay, C.A. No. 75-31-5 (N.D. Miss., July 28, 1977).

Mills v. Board of Education, 348 F. Supp. 866 (D.D.C. 1972).

National Labor Relations Board v. Detroit Edison, 560 F. 2d 722 (6th Cir. 1977).

Pennsylvania Association for Retarded Children v. Commonwealth of Pennsylvania, 334 F. Supp. 1257 (E.D. Pa. 1971).

Pierce v. Board of Education, 358 N.E. 2d 67 (Ill. App. 1976).

San Antonio Independent School District v. Rodriquez, 411 U.S. 1 (1973).

Shelton v. Tucker, 364 U.S. 479 (1960).

Stuart v. Nappi, 443 F. Supp. 1235 (D. Conn. 1978).

Tinker v. Des Moines, 393 U.S. 503 (1969).

About the Author

Reed Martin is an attorney with broad experience in law and education. After serving as legislative aide to United States Senator Ralph Yarborough, during his chairmanship of the Senate Health and Education Subcommittees, Mr. Martin spent 8 years in Washington. He performed education research under contract to 4 federal agencies and has consulted with over 100 schools and other facilities for the handicapped in 25 states. He has  conducted workshops on Educational Rights of Handicapped Children for school personnel in 12 states.

Mr. Martin now serves on the board of several advocacy organizations for the handicapped and on the education committee of the Houston Association for Retarded Citizens. Now located in Houston, where he directs the Public Law Division of Research Press, Mr. Martin has taught a course in Law and Psychology at the university level and has published widely. He writes the quarterly newsletter *Law and Behavior* and is the author of *Legal Challenges to Behavior Modification.*

181